11
TRADE SECRETS

TO CREATING A HIGH-PERFORMANCE DENTAL TEAM

11 TRADE SECRETS

TO CREATING A HIGH-PERFORMANCE DENTAL TEAM

SUSIE RASO

First published in 2022 by Dean Publishing
PO Box 119, Mt. Macedon, Victoria, 3441
Australia
deanpublishing.com

Copyright © Susie Raso

All rights reserved. No part of this publication may be reproduced, stored in a retrieval system or transmitted in any way or by any means, electronic, mechanical, photocopying, recording or otherwise, without the prior written permission of the author.

Cataloguing-in-Publication Data
National Library of Australia
Title: 11 Trade Secrets to Creating a High-Performance Dental Team
Edition: 1st edn
ISBN: 979-8-365200-41-8
Category: Business and Human Resources/Dentistry/Dental assistant

The information provided in this book is designed to provide helpful information on the subjects discussed. This book is not meant to be used, nor should it be used, to diagnose or treat any physical, emotional or psychological medical condition. For diagnosis or treatment of any medical problem, consult your own physician. The publisher and author are not responsible for any specific health or psychological needs that may require medical supervision and are not liable for any damages or negative consequences from any treatment, action, application or preparation, to any person reading or following the information in this book. References are provided for informational purposes only and do not constitute endorsement of any websites or other sources. Neither the publisher nor the individual author(s) shall be liable for any physical, psychological, emotional, financial, or commercial damages, including, but not limited to, special, incidental, consequential or other damages. Our views and rights are the same: You are responsible for your own choices, actions, and results.

CONTENTS

Introduction 7

Chapter 1: Have a Vision 19

Chapter 2: A Happy Team is a Powerful Asset........................... 25

Chapter 3: Your Environment Matters 49

Chapter 4: Building a Great Culture Conquers All 63

Chapter 5: Why Communicators
Are Smarter Than Everyone Else.. 81

Chapter 6: Getting Customer Service Right Every Time 103

Chapter 7: Building a High-Performance Mindset in Your Team ...117

Chapter 8: Solve These 9 Problems
and You Will Be Ahead of the Game 143

Chapter 9: Positive Self-Management and Team Management.... 163

Chapter 10: Leadership & Direction –
The Art of Moving Your Support Team Forward 169

Chapter 11: Why You Must Be Onboard with
the Holistic Movement in the Dental Industry 179

About the Author... 188

Acknowledgements 190

Endnotes... 192

INTRODUCTION

"Action is the foundational key to all success."
– *Pablo Picaso*

Congratulations on choosing to be part of a leading health industry. This book is full of inspiration, details every Practice Manager should know, and strategies for getting your team through tough times. I hope you are inspired by my story and how I got to be where I am today. You, too, can find your passion in an ever-changing industry that provides many learning opportunities.

When you are reading this book, you may feel you know it all already. However, push through. Even those who are experienced in the field still need to take on professional and personal development to enhance their skills and stay up to date. It is easy to become complacent and stagnant in your career when you feel you are on top of everything in your industry. However, there is always something to learn.

I am a wonderful example of this. At 42 years old, I am working as a Practice Manager for a large dental clinic in Melbourne's north. I knew from a very young age that I wanted to work as a Dental Assistant and I loved learning about teeth. My experience with Dentists was rewarding. This may seem odd to some people, but I have always wanted to work in this industry. The passion grew within me as I grew, and I knew that I would be one day at the top of my game, wanting to share this passion with anyone interested in hearing it.

IT STARTED WITH A MEMORY

"Do you know that an apple a day keeps the Dentist away?" the Dental Assistant asked with a smile. It was 1984 and I was a youngster with wayward curls and freckles.

The clang of the Dentist's instruments next to me faded into the background and I smiled back at the nice lady as my mind wandered. I wondered how many apples I could eat in a day. The drill started up and the Dentist asked me to open wide.

"Is orange your favourite colour?" the Dental Assistant asked me, nodding at my typical '80s fluoro t-shirt. Because I couldn't talk back, I just nodded slightly. I could smell the fluoride as the Dentist worked on my teeth, not that I knew what it was then. It is now an all-too-familiar scent in my current work. My body relaxed in the chair as the Dental Assistant continued to ask me questions and before I knew it, my appointment was over and I had not been scared one little bit!

That night when I got home, I told my mother about my dental experience and showed off my brand new orange Tek toothbrush, along with my "You have a wonderful smile" sticker. That evening, I ate seven apples in a row. I didn't feel so good later on. Nevertheless, I was extraordinarily happy, and it was from this point in my life that I promised myself I was going to be a Dental Assistant when I was older, and have a great smile.

As I grew up, I loved wearing makeup, putting on acrylic nails and choosing beautiful shoes to wear. I relished dressing up and feeling pretty. It was a part of my everyday life which I thoroughly enjoyed. My feelings about attending school, however, were quite the opposite. When I was a teenager, I would dream of leaving it for good. I hated it that much. When it came time to explore career paths in Year 9, a job as a Dental Assistant piqued my interest. A position at a dental practice seemed glamorous, just like being an airline steward. My childhood dental experiences were all positive. I fondly remembered the kindness and care of the Dentist and Dental Assistants and I wanted to be a part of that world.

I also loved communicating and helping people. It seemed the perfect fit to me.

I grew up in a loving and very supportive family. When I told my mum that I wanted to be a Dental Assistant, she could not be prouder. We never had private health insurance. Consequently, my experience was within the range of government-funded Oral Health Therapists and school dental vans. I am grateful for that, as I was inspired to similarly work in a practice that could help the average person who could perhaps not afford expensive dental care. It is what awakened a passion within me from the age of six.

In order to get into the dental industry, you need to have completed your Year 10 School Certificate and apply for a job traineeship. This was the pathway to become a qualified Dental Assistant. Despite my feelings about school, my mother wouldn't allow me to leave, citing that my potential wage would be greater if I had completed my Victorian Certificate of Education (VCE). I ended up failing Year 11 due to attendance because I hated school so much, but there was no option other than to persevere, so I repeated the year.

After completing VCE, the idea of being a Dental Assistant remained with me. After graduating, I took a leap of faith and looked for ANY job in the dental field. Rather than start small in a local dental practice, my world changed in 1996 when I ended up getting a job with a root canal specialist without any general dental experience at all.

OVERCOMING OBSTACLES TO REALISE A DREAM

I was given the opportunity to work for one of Melbourne's renowned Endodontic practices. It was quite difficult in the beginning. Dentistry, and particularly Endodontics, was a whole different world from what I knew. The pressure was on, and I felt that the Dental Assistants I worked alongside were mean to me. I was expected to learn every aspect of the job and workplace. I used to go home exhausted and stressed. I would cry most days and I felt so left out; I was the outsider and had to prove I was worthy of being a Dental Assistant.

Day in and day out, I tried and tried to understand what I was doing but I was struggling. I felt singled out and picked on. I had a meltdown and thought that surely I wasn't dreaming about my experience as a child being so positive. I then spoke with one of the senior team members and expressed how I was feeling. She was good enough to give me some pointers and I took them on board. I was determined to do well. I realised that all this time I had been complacent. Admittedly, I had a chip on my shoulder, and I was sending out a lot of negative energy. It fogged the brighter and bigger vision. I was not allowing myself to grow and absorb information. I had to learn the ropes to be able to live my childhood dream of being a Dental Assistant. Instead of focusing on the feeling that I was being picked on, I needed to change those thoughts to appreciation and gratitude about having an opportunity to find a job in the dental industry. I also needed to embrace the people I worked with, who were trying to train me while they were busy as well.

Unfortunately, there were aspects of the job I still had not grasped. I was approaching my three-month review, for which there was an upcoming meeting. I received my first written warning and it pointed out the areas I wasn't performing well in. I remember asking myself, *What do I have to do to show I am worthy of being a Dental Assistant?* My big girl dental gloves went on and I made a choice – it was time for me to step up or I was stepping out. To do that, I shut out everyone in my life except for my family so I could focus on work. I bought myself a notebook and coloured pens. I was determined to pursue and keep my job. It paid off; I was grasping the job better, referring to my notes and asking lots and lots of questions. There was no room for ongoing errors. I ensured I was eating healthily and that I was well-rested. I would go to bed earlier and rise early. I started work 30 minutes earlier to ensure my day was organised and well planned. I took the initiative to help the other team members and do more – I would take on extra tasks and soon enough I was on top of my game. My great attitude was infectious and became magnetic. I began to build relationships. I was loving work and working hard. I would even stay back to make sure the day's tasks were completed so there were no issues the following day. I wanted to do more and absorb more. I was a shining star running around the practice, performing the daily tasks and enjoying what I was doing.

FINDING MY NICHE

By 21 years old, I wanted to develop more skills and knowledge, and experience in a general dental clinic. I was blessed to have an opportunity to work in a Carlton North dental clinic and learn general dentistry. It was there that I became an A-grade Dental Assistant. A valuable team member mentored me in general dental procedures and we became great friends. We were a small, family-oriented dental clinic. There were two staff members and the Dentist. I studied my Certificate III in Dental Assisting and learnt forehand dentistry. I developed skills, gained knowledge and became a very efficient team player. I worked with dedication, pride and integrity. It was important to me to have the confidence of the client and be able to do my job well. I won hearts and trust, the clients were so thankful, and they enjoyed coming to the Dentist. I learnt key factors like not being judgmental, and took the time to get to know the client, treat them as an individual and not a number. It did not matter what their dental issues were, it was my duty to help them achieve their desired outcome, help shift their fear of coming to the Dentist, and make their time at the Dentist a humble and lovely experience.

One thing we did in order to make this happen was making muffins daily for the clients, and offering tea and coffee. Our mid-year functions and team-building events involved carrying out a working bee for the clinic's garden. I also remember once handing out pamphlets for our Dentist who was part of a council committee. The clinic would close for most of January and those who reached their KPIs would receive bonuses for their hard work.

When I started dental assisting, I found that my identity as a person was challenged. What I felt was a part of me (the makeup, nails and so forth) had to be stripped bare, exposing my vulnerability as a woman. I had to 'cut back' on what I thought I knew to be me, and begin to change to fit the role. I was determined though. I worked through my anxiety of being exposed within the realm of the Dental Assistant role and who I am. I pushed through understanding that this role was more than just the superficial makeup and nails. I realised that it was me who made me special. I persisted and worked through the anxiety and recognised this is what I wanted to do. I allowed the fear of being judged to be overruled by my ambition and dream to be in the industry.

I had to learn a whole new world of dentistry. I had to rediscover who I was. Learning and reading and following instruction, all with the passion and enthusiasm of a child. I knew this is where I was meant to be and felt so blessed to have taken the step to get it done.

Next came the part of learning. This learning took on a whole new meaning for me. Infection control was my thing, I loved it. I learned every bit, although I also understood that I had to be thorough. This was part of the job; I couldn't stuff this up! Too much was at risk. The operations for cross-contamination changed and I had to re-learn it all. I found that through this process, I was not only protecting myself, I was also protecting others. This made it feel more valuable and worth the effort. I learnt that the nitty gritty of the work can become overbearing and boring, but you must work through it. I cannot stress the importance of this enough.

I learned you must approach everything with a 'can-do' and proactive attitude. Find the joy in everything you do.

YOU ARE MORE THAN YOUR JOB

Through my work at many different practices and in various roles, I realised over the years that I was not JUST a Dental Assistant, I was integral to the success of the practice through the treatment outcome, the patient's wellbeing, and the Dentist's performance. I was the Dentist's communication partner. Often the Dentist speaks in a very technical manner, and the patient doesn't understand the terminology. I was there to bridge the gap. My innate intuition allowed me to anticipate the Dentist's every move, and to respond to unspoken patient questions. I was able to walk the patient through the process and create a seamless experience. I loved the win-win scenario of helping an anxious patient through the process and getting the dental outcome they desired. I did this by assisting them in understanding their treatment plan, getting them to look beyond their anxiety, and instilling them with confidence in their chosen Dentist.

I am now 42 years old and I have been fortunate to

be at my current dental practice for over 10 years (with the exception of a two-year break). I had left the dental industry to work within an RTO as a training consultant, delivering on-the-job traineeships in hospitality. Within a year, I knew I wanted to be back in the dental industry. The dental practice I had left had a policy of not rehiring anyone who had left, so I stayed where I was for the time being. However, I remained in contact with the Practice Principal, as we had had a great working relationship and friendship. Within two years the Practice Principal contacted me, telling me he needed my skillset to help take the practice through the next growth phase. He had found that since I had left the organisation, the remaining staff did not have the awareness or capacity to shift the practice from reactive to holistic. The extra administration had become stressful for him. I returned as the Hygiene Coordinator, then I moved up to the Clinical Coordinator role. Within two years, I became the Practice Manager.

HAVE A VISION

"Vision is the art of seeing the invisible."
— Jonathan Swift

In all industries, there are problems to overcome and the dental industry is no different. Here is a quick list of the problems I have seen and experienced in my years in the dental industry include:

- The influx of international Dental Assistants/ Hygienists/Dentists into Australia and the rising language and cultural barriers.

- Instruments are not being utilised to their full capacity anymore (that is, students know what a triplex water gun is, but they do not know how to use it).

- Changes to the Dental Assistant role – 20 years ago the Dental Assistant would be mixing the cements for the Dentist, whereas these days a lot of cements are premixed. Back then, if you did not get the consistency right, you could jeopardise the patient's outcome.

- Lack of cohesiveness between Dentists and Dental Assistants – there is less collaboration and passing of instruments to each other.

- The significance of infection control – Dental Assistants can find cleaning a chore, and this attitude can be lethal.

- Practice types have evolved from:
  » **Reactive** – which involves: fixing problems, having check-ups, high volume work, low cost; to
  » **Holistic** – which involves: proactive dental, higher treatment cost, less volume work, the practice is selling the Dentist time in the chair, more flow to practice.

This book is to help any Practice Principal or Practice Manager looking to grow their practice to successfully utilise the enthusiasm and skill set of its people, and help build rapport between staff and Dentist/patient dynamics.

CHAPTER 1

You may be:
- Considering buying an existing practice OR setting up a new practice.

- Purchasing an existing practice and resetting the vision, and consequently needing assistance to navigate existing staff.

- Recently promoted to Practice Manager and thus may be greener, rather than seasoned, (and would love to learn from another).

- Desiring to shift the practice success benchmark higher, including in terms of patient care and revenue.

- Changing the culture of a practice.

- Changing the direction of a practice.

For the purpose of the book, the term 'Practice Principal' refers both to the principal or owner.

Following the exercises included in this book will help you move your dental practice ahead of your competitors. For more information, go to thedentalconcierge.com.au.

ACTIVITY 1

Creating Your Vision

Think about the practice you currently own or manage, and before you dig into the book, jot down your initial thoughts:

- Where would I like the practice to be?

_____

_____

_____

_____

_____

_____

_____

CHAPTER 1

- What does that look like?

  _____

  _____

  _____

  _____

  _____

- What is the timeframe to achieve this?

  _____

  _____

  _____

  _____

  _____

  _____

2

A HAPPY TEAM IS A POWERFUL ASSET

> *"Teamwork is the ability to work together toward a common vision. The ability to direct individual accomplishments toward organizational objectives. It is the fuel that allows common people to attain uncommon results."*
> — **Andrew Carnegie**

WHY STAFF HAPPINESS IS IMPORTANT

The happiness of staff can never be underestimated. When staff are happy, they are likely to take on tasks that stretch their development, which will build their sense of achievement and confidence. When staff feel appreciated and valued, the flow-on is that lines of communication and team cohesiveness open up. Staff are happy to contribute wherever possible, and take any unforeseen changes in their stride. When a workplace is full of positive energy, staff enjoy being at work, and this trickles down through customer care, and the experience the customer receives.

HOW YOU CAN SUPPORT STAFF HAPPINESS

Managing staff can waver between joyful and tedious on any given day. This is dependent on your mood, any incidents that may occur, and the office dynamics. When it tips more often towards putting out fires and 'managing' people, rather than facilitating them to be the best they can be, it is time to reassess your style.

I have spent years undertaking personal development to feed my mind and improve my quality of life. The most surprising outcome has been understanding why people may respond or react the way they do, and these tools have impacted my people management skills tremendously. When you understand how each person ticks (the motivation that drives them), you will be able to contribute to their sense of significance and belonging in the workplace.

Needs

Tony Robbins is a huge influence in my life, and I had arranged for all staff to attend his 2020 Sydney Tour (which was unfortunately postponed due to COVID-19). From the staff who attended with me in 2019, I saw a huge leap in their personal development in the workplace.

CHAPTER 2

Tony talks of the 6 Human Needs which are broken down into the following:

1. **Certainty**: feeling safe and secure about the future.

2. **Variety**: the need for the unknown, change, new stimuli.

3. **Significance**: receiving recognition, to be needed.

4. **Connection**: a strong feeling of closeness or union with someone or something.

5. **Growth**: an expansion of capacity, capability or understanding.

6. **Contribution**: a sense of service and focus on helping, giving to and supporting others.

Knowing your staff are seeking the above six needs will help you see areas that are deficient if issues are arising.

ACTIVITY 2

See the needs

- What needs is the practice currently fulfilling?

  _____

  _____

  _____

  _____

  _____

- What could be improved upon?

  _____

  _____

  _____

  _____

  _____

- How could you contribute to the improvement?

Languages

The Five Love Languages by Dr Gary Chapman was released in 1992. While the original book outlined five different ways romantic partners express and experience love, the relationship language itself extends beyond closed doors into the workplace. Understanding of the languages in the workplace will help you motivate staff and create a culture in which staff are eager to come to work. I have included examples of how each primary language's needs can be expressed in a workplace to create a sense of belonging.

Words of Affirmation

Individuals whose primary language is Words of Affirmation thrive on hearing encouragement, compliments and praise.

Quality Time

Individuals with Quality Time as their primary language are happiest with the undivided attention of the people they are with, whether it is discussing work or a casual conversation at break.

Receiving Gifts

Individuals who have Receiving Gifts as their language thrive on the thoughtfulness and effort behind a gift. It can be as simple as buying them a chocolate bar, making them a coffee or bringing one in with you to work, or making a homemade cake to celebrate something.

Acts of Service
Individuals with Acts of Service as their primary language will greatly appreciate assistance in completing a task, or having someone complete a task for them when they are swamped or need to leave the office early.

Physical Touch
Individuals who speak this language thrive on physical touch. If they agree with the idea, high fives and pats on the back are a welcome acknowledgement of a job well done.

ACTIVITIES THAT FOSTER A SENSE OF BELONGING
Staff meetings
All-in staff meetings and team huddles are great ways to pull everyone together quickly. Staff meetings allow you to roll out information relating to the running of the practice and culture. Team huddles allow the team to connect, quickly address anything that arises, and be up-to-date on everyone's movements. Most workplaces will have monthly all-in staff meetings; I recommend a daily team huddle along with a weekly all-in staff meeting or department meetings, depending on your practice size.

ACTIVITY 3

Discover Team Languages

List each staff member and write down what you know their primary language to be.

Name: _____

Primary language: _____

Name: _____

Primary language: _____

Name: _____

Primary language: _____

Name: _____

Primary language: _____

Name: _____

Primary language: _____

CHAPTER 2

> How can you connect with each person in their language to increase their sense of belonging?
>
> Name: _____
>
> Ways to connect: _____
>
> Name: _____
>
> Ways to connect: _____
>
> Name: _____
>
> Ways to connect: _____
>
> Name: _____
>
> Ways to connect: _____
>
> Name: _____
>
> Ways to connect: _____
>
> Name: _____
>
> Ways to connect: _____

Regulatory training

Regulatory training ensures everyone in the organisation has been delivered the same information and sets the tone for what is and is not acceptable. Annual and new employee trainings include:

- Induction Training

- Work Health and Safety (WHS) Procedures and Policies:
  » Fire Safety – in particular, how to use a fire extinguisher
  » Slips, Trips and Falls
  » Hazardous Substances
  » Infection Control

- Wellbeing
  » Alcohol & Drugs
  » Bullying in the Workplace
  » Occupational Violence and Aggression

There are a number of accredited organisations that can deliver training at your premises.

Team-building activities

In my experience, hands-on team-building activities (with lots of laughter) greatly contribute to each person's sense of belonging, not only within the organisation, but within their team. It is a chance to interact with others who they may not work with on a daily basis.

Events held offsite help add to the overall team atmosphere and aid social interaction. Being away from the workplace allows staff to relax, interact, and absorb new skills on another level.

Team-building events can come in various forms, including:
- Tree Ropes/Ziplining
- Amazing Race
- Escape Room
- Axe Throwing
- Sailing
- Bubble Soccer
- Scavenger Hunt
- Charity Events – Billy Carts for Kids, Toys for Kids, Bike Building, Robot Wars, Lego Challenge

Regular 1:1s | Staff development plan

When interviewing staff, discover their desired career path and span. During their probation period, check in regularly to see what it is they are enjoying and advise that you will delve into their career development plan on completion of their probation. Rather than creating a development plan

ACTIVITY 4

Brainstorm some team-building activities your team may enjoy.

_____

_____

_____

_____

_____

_____

_____

_____

_____

_____

straight away, I recommend seeing what they can do first. I have experienced firsthand a misalignment between what someone's CV outlines, what they say they can do in the interview, and how they show up daily.

You should endeavour to meet individually with each staff member to discuss and review their career progression and understand their personal needs. Then you can help put into place a plan for their continued professional development, as well as for the organisation's growth (this could include adding new staff and/or services). It is an opportunity for staff to freely voice their preference and any concerns or feedback in their outlined direction. At each one-to-one, I recheck their intended industry lifespan and whether their career path has changed. People's circumstances (including health, matrimony, family) change quickly, and knowing how to support them during times of uncertainty fosters their sense of belonging.

Regular one-to-ones enhance a sense of belonging through:

- **Employee retention** – staff are loyal when they feel nurtured and supported in growing personally and professionally.

- **Building staff morale** – staff with a sense

of belonging will enjoy working in a positive, motivated, and committed workforce.

Regular meetings ensure you are open and approachable, and the staff member feels they are a valuable member of the team.

Technical training & personal development

Through the staff development plan and regular one-to-one discussion, you are able to adjust the learning development pathway for the individual. Do they need further technical skills? Do they need to build their soft skills, (for example, communication such as listening or articulating, creative thinking, problem solving, conflict management, delegation, team player, flexibility)? Are they taking longer to reach their target than initially discussed? (If so, what is going on that is affecting this? Lack of confidence? Distractions at home?). If they *are* at that level, are they looking to grow quickly and what can be fast-tracked? Tailoring training to each individual based on their strengths and areas of improvement lifts the individual up, enhancing their self-worth. Knowing the organisation has their back and allows team members to utilise and develop their skill set.

Social occasions

Whether onsite or offsite, any of the following activities encourages individuals to socialise outside of their direct team and enhance their sense of belonging.

Morning or afternoon teas to celebrate staff celebrations:
- Milestone anniversaries (five years, 10 years, etc)
- Practice anniversaries
- Engagements
- Weddings
- Birth of a child
- Farewells
- Retirement

Social (onsite) ideas:
- Morning teas/lunches to raise funds for charity – everyone brings a plate and contributes money to raise funds.

- Holidays/Religious Holidays – team lunch and everyone brings in a plate themed to an occasion, i.e. Australia Day, Valentine's Day, St Patrick's Day, Pancake Day, Greek Easter, Fourth of July, Halloween, Melbourne Cup luncheon, Hanukkah, etc.

ACTIVITY 5

Make a list of each team member and make a list of skills or training that would benefit them.

Name: _____

Skill/training: _____

_____

_____

Name: _____

Skill/training: _____

_____

_____

Name: _____

Skill/training: _____

_____

_____

CHAPTER 2

Name: _____

Skill/training: _____

_____

_____

_____

Name: _____

Skill/training: _____

_____

_____

_____

Name: _____

Skill/training: _____

_____

_____

Social (offsite) ideas:
- Team lunch once a month at the local pub, cafe, club or restaurant.

- Christmas celebration with Bad Santa or Kris Kringle.

TEAM HAPPINESS AND JOY BUILDS A TEAM THAT PERFORMS

In October of 2019, the University of Oxford found that happy workers are more productive.[1] It makes sense that any workplace with happy employees will experience more productivity and a dental practice is no different. It is also important to note that the amount of stress employees experience will vary depending on the industry in which they work.

Many Dentists and staff experience moderate to severe stress levels in practice. One study shows that 79% of Dentists experience moderate/severe stress![2] That's a whopping number. Another similar study found the number to be closer to 86%.[3]

If employees are under significant stress, it is perhaps even more vital to focus on creating a happy workplace in order to support them and decrease their stress levels.

What does team happiness look like? To me, the workplace is a positive, cohesive place where people are naturally supportive, helpful and appreciative.

What does it feel like? Staff have a sense of belonging (they see their colleagues as their 'work family'), there is purpose, integrity, equality, and a rhythm of connectivity and gratitude that flows to the customer. The role of the Practice Manager is orchestrating the flow of the practice, so it encompasses all of the above.

When the practice does not include all these elements, it is up to the Practice Manager to nip the negativity in the bud to stop it infiltrating the workplace daily. Encourage those being negative to speak up to you, their supervisor or manager, and never down to colleagues. It is important to stress that what one person thinks may not be what the other person is doing or thinking.

Have those difficult conversations that will stop a bitch-fest dead in its tracks. Handle grievances and even terminate staff, if the need arises. With any grievance, the Practice Manager will need to meet with those involved, be direct and patient with their responses and underlying reasons, and keep the lines of communication open. Bring the conversation back to philosophy of practice, remind the employee to speak UP not down, and discuss whether there is a language difference or cultural difference that will help the individual be more solution-focused in future. Remember to document any grievances as per the practice's policy.

TOP TIPS FOR CONNECTING WITH STAFF
Be honest
Understanding an individual's personal life will assist in the workplace, whether it is related to happiness, new experiences or anxiety and stress. Be honest and open with staff when having a conversation, and remind them that they are accountable, to ensure their behaviour falls within practice guidelines. If they are experiencing cultural differences (a lessening of boundaries) such as partying or taking recreational drugs, check that it is not impacting their performance at work. (Are they tired from being out at all hours? Are they still under the influence)?

If you as the Practice Manager experience a misunderstanding or make a mistake and fail to pick it up, take responsibility and talk about it at your team huddle. This will demonstrate your authenticity and your team will understand that you are only human too. Sometimes you will need to discuss your own life to allow others to connect with you.

Spontaneous coffees
Spontaneous one-to-ones, by means of a coffee catch up, help greatly when you need to take someone out of the workspace for a conversation to see how they are going. It allows them to be candid if something is worrying them

or if they need someone to bounce ideas off. If you have staff from different cultural backgrounds, it gives them the space to ask you questions they may be embarrassed to ask you in the practice. Don't have a coffee shop nearby? Grab them a coffee on the way to work and have a chat in the carpark. Alternatively, take a 10-minute walk away from prying eyes and ears.

The three most common reasons staff members are in my office are:
- They want one-to-one time
- They are 'in trouble'
- They are there to complain

Take the time to integrate new employees

Investing the time with new employees will save you time in the long run. Do they need training on any software or procedures? Do they need training on any equipment? Do they need to unlearn a skill to relearn it in a more time-efficient way? Is there anything they are unsure of? Utilise this time to tap into their learning style and speak 'their language'.

Delegating responsibilities

If a staff member has identified something that could be improved within a process or the practice, and it is something that will be a positive contribution, ask them if they would be willing to implement it. It allows them to take responsibility for something, to build their confidence and to take ownership.

Create a 'work family' environment

Building a 'work family' environment where you feel needed and belong is a place people will want to come to and contribute to daily. Consider how staff can contribute to the work family environment as well. Use humour to bring a smile to everyone's face. When I installed a swipe card reader in the practice, I named the reader 'Kevin' and added a bow tie! How can you not smile and say hello to Kevin each time you go through the door?

ACTIVITY 6

List some ways you can connect with the team and add some personal touches into the workplace.

_____

_____

_____

_____

_____

_____

_____

_____

_____

_____

3

YOUR ENVIRONMENT MATTERS

> *"You are a product of your environment.
> So choose the environment that will best
> develop you toward your objective.
> Analyze your life in terms of its environment.
> Are the things around you helping you toward
> success — or are they holding you back?"*
> **– W. Clement Stone**

CREATING A CALM AND WELCOMING PRESENCE

RECEPTION/PATIENT WAITING AREA

The reception/patient waiting area is your patient's first impression of your practice. It only takes seconds to form an impression. How you make an impact in those seconds is what has your patients choosing to continue with their appointment, return for future dental work and recommend your practice to others.

Take a look at your reception/patient waiting area. What sensory experience does it offer, and what does it say about the practice and the people who work there? Is it: cool and fresh; cold; warm and welcoming; overly clinical and sterile; disorganised and cluttered; or tired and in need of a refresh?

Swap roles and become the patient. Experience the practice through their eyes. The following will help guide you as you audit the practice.

PATIENT CHECK-IN/CHECK-OUT
Welcoming and friendly environment

What do your patients experience the moment they step into reception? Eye contact and a warm smile? Are they acknowledged by name (if a long-term patient) and asked how they are doing?

On arrival, ask the patient if any of their details have changed since their last appointment. Not only does this keep the files up-to-date, it adds a personalised touch. Adding notes to the client file (whether in the 'We Know You' section or 'Pop Up' notes) ensures all staff have a patient's requirements at their fingertips to make customers feel extra special and well-cared for.

Examples of notes may include:
- Mrs Jones is elderly and requires assistance getting in/out of the taxi.

- Mr Brown has been a patient of 20 years and enjoys a long black coffee.

- Ms Andrews has anxiety around dental procedures.

- Do not use lidocaine with Mr Citizen.

Is the check-in counter free of clutter? A neat and tidy space will instill confidence in the customers that the workplace is organised and sanitary. This is important in most workplaces but even more so at a dental practice, where people expect outstanding hygiene and service.

If you have patients who have been coming to you for many years, you will find they enjoy having a chat with you, especially if you have been there for many years also. The administration staff are the face of the business; they are the ones the patients connect with most. Take the time to take an interest in them.

If you find a staff member who is not as warm and welcoming as you would like, they may lack confidence to connect. For instance, they may not know how to interact with kids; they may never have dealt with an overly anxious person before; and so on. Sit with them, discuss examples of clients with different personalities and the best way to converse with them.

Patient privacy

When a treatment plan has been pulled together, is there a space to hold the discussion so the patient can discuss their concerns, treatment options and/or payment plans?

When booking appointments over the phone and to make sure nothing is missed, it is best the Front Desk staff have a set list of questions to ask and ensure the patient information is up-to-date. With new patients, it is critical to gather as much information as possible to find out what it is they are looking for. See whether the practice is able to meet their needs, and whether the patient is a right fit for the practice. I created a specific tool to discover this; it is called the New Patient Discovery Call Sheet. This sheet helps new staff learn the job requirements.

Ambience

What feeling or mood does the practice currently have?

Can anything be improved? These areas are key to a patient's experience. Tune into your customers when they enter the room to try and interpret this. You may also like to make note of any feedback they give, whether formal or informal.

Scent

What is the scent of the practice when you enter? Does it smell clinical? Is there a fragrance smell? Is it artificial or strong and may irritate sensitive noses? Are there flowers in an arrangement that can irritate allergy sufferers? All of these elements need to be taken into account to ensure the customer has an optimal experience.

Sound

If you are waiting in reception, what do you hear? Is there music playing? Music can assist with toning down the phone conversations and softly played music of a calming nature can help decrease anxiety for patients. Music/genre suggestions include acoustic, chill out, spa, classical – depending on style of practice and/or clientele. At my first dental practice we only played ABC classical music, the second practice was jazz (that is, Frank Sinatra and Dean Martin). Some practices like to play the Top 40, however it is important to ensure the language used is appropriate for people of all ages.

Temperature

What is the room temperature of reception? A room that is too hot or too cool (depending on the season) can detract from the experience. The ideal temperature is between 25 to 27°C for cooling in summer, and around 18 to 22°C for heating in winter. (I would aim for 22°C for areas where floors are non-carpeted). Are the units adequate for the floor space? It can be hard to strike a balance that pleases everyone. To solve this, you might like to include some additional blankets in the reception area.

Furniture

Is there a variety of different seating arrangements? Are the chairs comfortable? Are the sofas easy to get out of? Have you considered the needs of young children and elderly patients? You could add some armless chairs, and ensure there is space for patients with ability aids.

Flooring

Small changes can make all the difference in the look and feel of a practice (including a new coat of paint). Does the flooring meet your needs?

If the practice has carpet:
- Are you able to clean up spills easily? Is it stained? Does it need to be steam cleaned on a regular basis?

- Is it looking tired and worn?

Entertainment

Are there patients who turn up early to their appointment?
What about when the Dentist is running late?
What do patients do while they wait?

Firstly, let us take a look around the room:
- Do you have the current edition of magazines on the table? (I always get great feedback that we always have the current edition on the table.)

- Do the patients have access to water?

- Is the kids' area visible and at one end of the waiting room?

- What do you have in the way of entertainment for kids? If this includes toys, can they be easily sanitised?

Feature items such as fish tanks, sculpture art and wall art enhance the patients' sensory experience, as well as adding value to the general perception of the space. Hiring these pieces allows you to change them up after a certain period of time to give a fresh look to the practice.

Fish tanks are a wonderful addition; not only are they entertaining for kids, but they generally create a sense of calm for patients. A 2019 study observed that live fish improve perceptions of mood, relaxation and anxiety.[4]

Refreshments for patients

Invest in a coffee machine. I have had clients arrive early just so they can have time out and a tea or coffee before their appointment. Place a menu on the counter or in the waiting area.

Cleanliness

Aside from the policies governed by the Dental Association Infection Control Guidelines:

- Are the floors cleaned daily – that is, vacuumed or mopped?

- Are the floors clear of stains or scuff marks?

- Are the walls clear of scuff marks?

- Are the walls in need of a fresh coat of paint? A new layer of paint will give a crisp fresh appearance.

- Are wastepaper baskets emptied daily?

- Are there used glasses and coffee cups left unattended in the waiting area?

- Are the windows free of marks (usually from children) on the inside, and clean on the outside?

- Are the magazines displayed on the table?

- Is the furniture wiped down/sanitised regularly?

- Has the necessary sanitisation been updated to reflect the current policies?

- What is your COVID plan?

CONNECTING WITH THE CUSTOMER
Feedback
Have you implemented the following as part of your patient care?

- SMS and email reminders, as well as phone call reminders for elderly clients with landline numbers only.

- Post-treatment survey.

- SMS check in follow-up.

- Phone call follow-up (either related to treatment or responding to an enquiry).

Following up post-treatment reassures the patient they are in the best care. Having a patient know you have their best interests at heart is gold! It is far easier to retain your existing clients than it is to find new clients.

Social media channels

Do you use social media to your advantage to connect to clients and potential clients? I have used social media to:

- Share practice updates such as new procedures.

- Notify changes to practice trading restrictions (during COVID-19).

- Connect and share premise changes, such as removing carpets and installing floorboards.

- Connect through photos of the team, photos from onsite wellbeing seminars, photos of team-building days.

Are you connecting with your clients on social media?

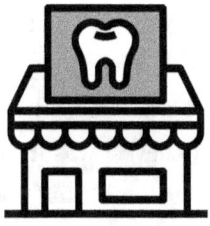

IN THE CLINIC

The clinic's policies and procedures will be based around the relevant Dental Association Infection Control Guidelines. I am including the additional key considerations below. As per the reception/front desk area, cleanliness and patient comfort (including temperature) flows into the clinic space.

Signage

Are the exit signs labelled clearly? Are the clinic rooms labelled and easy to see? Are the restrooms easy for patients to find?

Safety

Are all staff aware of those with the appropriate medical training (for example, who is the first aid officer, and so on)?

Does everyone know how to use a fire extinguisher and where the evacuation point is? In one of my previous career experiences in hospitality, the oven caught on fire.

I found the fire extinguisher but I had no idea how to pull the pin or use it. I eventually pulled the pin and it worked (thankfully). I was shocked to find myself in that situation. I couldn't believe I was in that situation; it was extremely stressful, and I still talk about it to this day. I would hate for any staff member to not know what to do if there was an incident involving a fire. Fire extinguisher training has been and must continue to be implemented in the workplace.

Patient comfort

Ensure the room is at the ideal temperature for the season, and that there are additional pillows and blankets in each room. Pillows and blankets provide warmth and comfort. In a dental practice, where many people have anxiety surrounding their visit, this sensory addition is even more important and welcome. Likewise, diffusing essential oils in the waiting area and providing stress balls could also make a difference to the stress levels of patients.

Industry trends

Is the practice staying up to date with current industry trends and innovation? Has training been undertaken by all involved? This includes keeping administration staff updated on new procedures so they can explain and answer any questions from patients.

CHAPTER 3

Susie is sharing bonus material.

Visit thedentalconcierge.com.au/book-bonuses

4

BUILDING A GREAT CULTURE CONQUERS ALL

"Culture is simply a shared way of doing something with a passion."
– Brian Chesky

What does a family-feel work culture look like? It is where everybody respects every other team member, not only for the contribution of their workload and the smooth running of the organisation, but also how they add to the collective harmony of the group dynamics through social and cultural interactions. It is an environment where everyone feels confident and secure to be the best they can be, and to provide that encouragement to others also.

Before we explore building a great culture more deeply, take a moment to complete this activity:

ACTIVITY 7

A culture audit

- What is the current culture of our practice?

  _____

  _____

- Does anything need to change? List possible changes.

  _____

  _____

  _____

- If so, what would I like the culture of the practice to be?

  _____

  _____

We will revisit these questions at the end of the chapter.

CHAPTER 4

BUILDING A WARM, FAMILY-FEEL WORK CULTURE

The following are the key building blocks for a culture that fosters personal growth, organisational growth and harmony.

VALUES OF AN ORGANISATION

Off the top of your head, do you know the values of the organisation? My guess is you do, because as Practice Manager you live and breathe them. But what about the remaining staff? Do they know them? Do they embody them? Is a list of the values posted in areas where staff congregate, such as the kitchen?

Values, I believe, that are key to any organisation are: integrity, care/empathy/compassion, respect, innovation, diversity and self-awareness/improvement.

Never underestimate the power of words. Naming what you want to see in your organisation and displaying those words for your staff to regularly see can have a positive impact. Words can motivate and inspire. One thing that has remained with me from high school was the motto '*Quantum potes, tantum aude*', which translates to 'Dare to do as much as you are able'. If the repetition of such phrases in our schooling can leave such a mark, (even when in Latin!), we cannot underestimate the power they can have in the workplace as well.

When was the last time you reviewed the organisation's values? If it was a while ago, do they still align with the organisation and culture? You will notice if it is out of alignment when you look at what issues keep presenting themselves for your patients and staff. If your instinct is telling you that it is time to update the values of the organisation, follow this quick activity on the next page to see whether they need a tweak or a reboot.

Do the existing values need small changes or an overhaul? Have a discussion with the Practice Principal. If a reboot is in order, then collaborate and repeat the above exercise at a staff meeting or staff development day. Why is this important? Because staff will get on board more easily if there are values that align with their own. There is also more chance that they will take ownership of the values because they contributed to setting them. As a consequence, the staff may feel empowered and valued because they have had a say in how the organisation will move forward.

Creating Team Values

Grab a whiteboard or place a large piece of butcher's paper on a wall to use. You may wish to print out copies of a shortened list of values (about 50) to hand out. For larger practices, split staff into pairs or small groups. For smaller practices, have them do the task

ACTIVITY 8

A values audit

- What are the current values of the practice (spoken and unspoken)?

  _____

  _____

  _____

  _____

- Do these values fit the future growth of the practice or do they need to be updated?

  _____

  _____

  _____

  _____

  _____

individually. Allow them five to 10 minutes to prioritise the individual's/group's top three values. Once the time is up, ask staff to call out what they think should be included in the top 10 values and why. Write them down on the whiteboard or paper, and through a process of elimination, whittle it down to 10 values. Once everyone is in agreement for the top 10, decide which five to six values are the most important. The remaining four to five will ultimately be secondary values.

You can even be creative in how you present your values, just as Atlassian (a successful software development company) did:

- Open company, no bullshit

- Build everything with heart and balance

- Don't #@!% the customer

- Play as a team

- Be the change you seek[5]

CONSIDERING DIVERSITY

People can have vastly different cultural experiences, even if they grow up in the same country. For example, there would be a huge contrast between the lifestyle of someone from outback Australia to that of a city slicker. Immigrant staff may bring different cultural and/or religious experiences with them and possibly the added difficulty of cross-cultural communication if speaking English as a second language. Whether traditional versus modern religious values, gender equality versus traditional gender roles, alternative body language or words used, these elements all come under the banner of diversity. Do not make assumptions about a person based on their cultural or religious background. Rather, in your next conversation with them, find out what it was like for them growing up. Celebrate diversity through themed staff luncheons and promote acceptance via education. This may mean being aware of a staff member's religious festivals, so that you may greet them appropriately on the day, or learning basic sign language for a staff member who has a hearing impairment, for example.

EVERYONE IS A LEADER

In any role, aided by systems and guidelines, you develop a rhythm with your work. This rhythm expands

ACTIVITY 9

Making your values work for you

- Select 10 values that you believe are important to the practice and write them below.

1.

2.

3.

4.

5.

6.

7.

8.

9.

10.

*Scan the QR code to view the List of Organisational Values for ideas. Make sure you identify what it means to the organisation.

- Prioritise the values in the order you feel is most important.

- Narrow this list down to five to six core values.

1.

2.

3.

4.

5.

6.

www.thedentalconcierge.com.au/book-bonuses

to the team as the individuals sync with each other. As a result, the group forms a harmonious rhythm. When the rhythm is out of alignment, the flow of the team and outcome becomes affected. Fostering proactivity and leadership not only helps the individual and the team, it helps enhance problem solving, confidence and leadership skills. When everyone takes responsibility for the outcome, it is easier to have a conversation with the person(s) involved to find out what happened. That is, have they been shown how to do a task, did they need help, were the instructions clear, and so forth. Problem solving encourages team cohesion and collaboration through identifying system improvements. It can often also result in a win-win situation by lifting the team member up, enhancing the team flow, and improving the organisation.

Encourage the team to be proactive instead of reporting an incident directly to management every time something happens. Reinforce that small grievances can be handled by each team and that management can step in if escalation is required. The benefit is streamlining the system to work better for everyone; there is less downtime due to inefficiency; and it is confidence building for those involved. Role play the new procedure and common scenarios at a staff training day.

ACTIVITY 10

Proactive approach

- What instances can you encourage staff to facilitate a proactive approach?

  _____

  _____

  _____

- What role plays could you implement to help the team implement a proactive approach.

  _____

  _____

  _____

  _____

  _____

For example:

1. Identify an incident.

2. Approach the person(s) involved.

3. Using neutral body language and tone, open up a conversation to see what happened and whether they need assistance.

4. Ask them what they can do if it occurs again. If they are unsure, work together to come up with a plan (seeking assistance from a team leader where needed).

5. Validate the outcome, tweak if necessary, and update any system or policy guidelines.

6. Share the occurrence, and seek collaboration/ support and outcome at the next staff meeting for others to learn from.

STAFF MEETINGS

Regular team huddles allow the team to address any personal or operating issues that arise, and to handle them quickly. All-in staff meetings then have the space to focus on the direction of the practice, and identify short- to long-term goals.

The benefits of regular staff meetings include:

1. **Giving feedback** – space for all team members to contribute about what is and is not working.

2. **Problem-solving** – the ability to problem-solve, on the spot, any feedback about things that are not working.

3. **Being able to pivot** – ability to make changes without losing vast quantities of time, energy or money.

4. **Building skills** – learn from others and stretch comfort zones to embrace new skills.

5. **Sharing positivity** – start the day with collaboration and fire everyone up!

I have found the following agenda structure adds to the collaborative culture, and that when you rotate the parts of the meeting around staff conduct, it helps build their confidence.

- Positive feedback first – phone messages; customer ratings from surveys, SMS follow-up, social media; and positive comments/shout outs between staff on their performance

- General housekeeping

- Upcoming events

- Practice updates

I have run monthly staff meetings before, but have found the sweet spot is more than once a month. I recommend either of the following:
- Weekly meetings – suggested for new practices, new teams or when connectivity is required; or

- Fortnightly meetings – for mature practices and seasoned teams.

When a task has been assigned to a staff member, weekly meetings make for an easy update and completion date. A month is too long a time to await feedback and will not have as positive an effect. Block out the booking calendar for the duration of the meeting to ensure attendance by all. If for any reason someone is absent, bring them up to date at their next arrival into the workplace to make sure everyone is fully informed at all times.

REFLECTING ON HOW YOU OPERATE

COVID-19 has forced practices (and many businesses) to change the way they operate, whether through reduced staff, reduced trading hours, or infection control. It has provided an opportunity to reflect on what does and does not work for the practice and staff and to pivot if needed. For example, the practice I currently manage has changed its trading hours to Monday to Thursday, from 8:00 am until 5:30 pm. All staff are in attendance those days, which creates consistency, and there are the added benefits of everyone gaining an extra day of personal time, and no-one working weekends. How good is that? Three-day weekends!

ACTIVITY 11

Reflect on your meetings

- Are staff meetings regularly scheduled?

  _____

- Does the current schedule work or does it need to be changed?

  _____

- What is the general attitude to staff meetings?

  _____

  _____

  _____

  _____

Tip: Set up a meeting schedule and list staff who will be chairing or conducting parts of the meeting (Ensure all staff have a turn at some point).

ACTIVITY 12

Reflecting on the operations

- Reflecting on the practice operation, is there anything you would consider changing?

_____

_____

_____

_____

- What changes would benefit the business?

_____

_____

_____

_____

_____

5

WHY COMMUNICATORS ARE SMARTER THAN EVERYONE ELSE

"If everyone is moving forward together, then success takes care of itself."
– **Henry Ford**

THE POWER OF EFFECTIVE COMMUNICATION

The natural ability to small talk or being able to converse easily is not the same thing as effective communication. The 'gift of the gab' for small talk and conversations with colleagues helps others feel comfortable around you. However, when it comes to explaining what is required, motivating staff and ensuring delivery outcomes, it is an entirely different type of communication that is needed.

Before we look at communicating with others, let us first look at how we are communicating with ourselves. The words we say (spoken both aloud and inwardly) are a great indicator of where our mindset is at. Truly listen to what someone is saying; it is the window to their default mindset. Are they an optimistic, glass half-full person, or a pessimistic, glass half-empty type of person? Do they embrace change easily? Are they willing to try new things? Do they jump in and get on with the job, or do they drag their feet?

In the table opposite are examples of negative phrases that may arise and suggestions to help to reframe them more positively:

CHAPTER 5

Negative, self-defeating	Positive, empowering
I should …	I will …
I'm not able to do this!	I'll give it a go!
I don't know how.	Who knows, who can assist me?
I can't …	What can I do here?
It's impossible!	What else is possible?
It's not my fault!	I'm response-able
I'm no good at ….	What I can do is …
Why does this always happen to me?	What can I change here to stop this from happening again?
I'm stupid.	I messed up and it's okay. What's the lesson here?

ACTIVITY 13

Communication

- What negative phrases do you hear regularly in the practice? List the most common issues.

_____

_____

_____

_____

_____

_____

_____

_____

- What positive phrases do you hear regularly in the practice? List the most common.

_____

_____

_____

_____

_____

_____

_____

_____

_____

_____

_____

To begin changing mindset and culture, start at staff meetings by setting up a quote for the week for all to embody. The quote can be printed out and stuck by the kettle, on the refrigerator door and back of the staff restroom door as a reminder.

Examples could be:

> *We are not a team because we work together.*
> *We are a team because we respect,*
> *trust and care for each other.*
> **– Vala Afshar**

> *Successful people build each other up.*
> *They motivate, inspire and push each other.*
> *Unsuccessful people just hate, blame and complain.*
> **– Anonymous**

> *Teamwork divides the tasks*
> *and multiplies the success.*
> **– Unknown**

> *The strength of the team is each individual member.*
> *The strength of each member is the team.*
> **– Phil Jackson**

CHAPTER 5

*Ability is what you're capable of doing.
Motivation determines what you do.
Attitude determines how well you do it.*
– **Lou Holtz**

*The nice thing about teamwork is that
you always have others on your side.*
– **Margaret Carty**

*Don't limit yourself. Many people limit themselves
to what they think they can do. You can go as far
as your mind lets you. What you believe,
remember, you can achieve.*
– **Mary Kay Ash**

Do one thing every day that scares you.
– **Eleanor Roosevelt**

LEARNING STYLES

Each person understands information differently. Knowing their primary 'language' will help you to have effective conversations and share office updates. Not everyone falls under a single category; many people often span two or three. However, one will be their primary language. When having a one-to-one conversation with an individual, you would focus on their primary language. When addressing the office as a group, you would ensure your message contained all languages present in the office.

People communicate, learn and understand information in one of five ways. These 'learning styles' can be defined as: auditory, auditory digital, hands-on/kinesthetic, visual, and reading/writing.

Auditory

Auditory individuals enjoy hearing the information and actively participate in discussions. They may repeat what you said, and tend to remember spoken examples rather than written words.

An auditory person will use the following words in their speech: "Can you hear. . .?", "That sounds good", "Listen. . .", "That rings a bell", "It resonates", "How does that sound?"

Auditory Digital

Auditory digital individuals show symptoms of other learning styles which may be harder to spot initially. They understand by creating or learning steps, systems and procedures.

An auditory digital person will use the following words

in their speech: *sense, understand, think, consider, change, perceive, know*, "Does that make sense?".

Hands-On/kinesthetic

Hands-On/kinesthetic individuals prefer to undertake hands-on activities or use their senses to understand what you are saying. They may doodle their notes, gesture when speaking, and think and engage better when moving (for example, tapping their foot).

A hands-on/kinesthetic person will use the following words in their speech: *feel, touch, grasp, get a hold of, tap into, concrete, solid*, "Do you have a handle on it?".

Visual

Visual individuals prefer to see information you are discussing. That is, draw a diagram on a whiteboard, see a picture, view a presentation or watch a video.

A visual person will use the following words in their speech: *see, look, appear, view, show me, imagine*, "Get the picture?".

Reading/writing

Reading/writing individuals absorb information through written words and making notes and lists. They will order things into priorities and have lots of information in their spoken sentences.

If you see that someone does not understand, rephrase what you are saying in their 'language and interests' to get the message across. For example, I have a staff member who is into music and dance. I refer to what I know of them and apply it in the workplace when their mind and body language says they are not able to do it. "Just think of yourself at a rave where you're in free flow. If you were in free flow doing this task, what would you do?"

COMMUNICATION PROBLEMS IN THE DENTAL INDUSTRY

SAME TECHNICAL SKILL, DIFFERENT WAYS OF WORKING

In preparation for restrictions lifting during COVID-19, a team meeting between Hygienists and therapists was held regarding the need to streamline procedures, in particular the use of high suction. Half of the team were requesting a Dental Assistant for the procedure which puts pressure on auxiliary staff, affects the operation, and in the long run, costs the practice more money. I used my experience in the role to open the conversation to get to the core of the issue:

CHAPTER 5

"You know, when I was the Hygiene Coordinator for the Hygienist I wasn't in the room for these procedures, and I need to understand why you need somebody in the room. What are the differences here?"

I discovered their training was different – 10 plus years ago, Hygienists were trained to work on their own with little assistance. In the practice we had Hygienists whose performance was either tactile (self-sufficient, able to troubleshoot themselves, they remained calm) or visual (needed to stay focused on what they were doing with an assistant to support them, without assistance they were prone to stress). Once each side understood the differences, they solved the problem together. The outcome: a change in equipment for each staff member.

SAME TRAINING, DIFFERENT SKILL LEVEL

Communication problems can arise between staff of the same qualification. For example, some Dental Assistants have been trained in the same units but are at different skill levels. One may be more skilful and coordinated, while another may have had less opportunity to practice, reinforce their learnings, and build their confidence.

PERCEPTION GAPS

Miscommunication can be due to differences in tenure, on the job skills, and previous practice experience.

Someone who has worked in a small practice with two rooms and a high volume of patients may have had more exposure than someone who has been in a larger practice. Then there are staff who have been in the industry for a long time, when dental infection control standards were not as high. Compare this to a younger Dentist who has had infection control at the centre of their training. We cannot know the experience of each individual unless we ask and have open, non-judgemental conversations.

HOW TO PREVENT COMMUNICATION BREAKDOWNS

There will be staff who share the same complaints, such as, "They do nothing", "They don't think for me", where you need to anticipate their needs. And others who say, "They don't communicate", "They don't keep the patient calm", and so on. Some staff may not feel confident and do not understand the impact of their role/actions. They may not know how to communicate with an anxious patient. They may fear expressing themselves. Investing time in the work 'family' culture and building soft skills will help open up communication. Let us address these common communication breakdowns.

For the individual stating "They do nothing" and "They don't think for me", have them practice telling the other staff member what it is they need. This way they can check whether the communication they are using is clear. Then, through repetition, the workflow is being reinforced and becomes a habit. For some, to anticipate another's needs does not come naturally to them and they need to learn this soft skill.

For the individual who is not communicating, have them practice talking throughout the procedure to the other staff member in the room. They can tell them what they are doing in order to be clear about where they are at. From my experience when I was working in smaller teams and taking on more responsibilities, there was no choice but to communicate "While you're numbing up, I'm just going to quickly go do these instruments".

To teach how to keep a patient calm, I suggest role playing different scenarios that may arise. The staff member may be a visual learner and need to see a scenario in action in order to learn and draw upon that knowledge at a later date.

It is also important to be mindful of the staff you pair together for work. There will be a difference in rapport between pairings of new staff members, who may be still finding their groove working together, compared to pairings of seasoned staff members, who may be more comfortable with each other.

Take a look at the personality dynamics in pairings and team dynamics per patient and procedure. Perhaps you need to switch the Dental Assistant depending on the procedure. If you have someone who is newer to the industry, is there the capacity for them to shadow another on procedures they are not confident in?

Above all, use humour to help people relax and open up.

WHAT TO DO WHEN THERE IS A MISCOMMUNICATION

When miscommunication is unable to be resolved by those involved and it escalates, I have found the following procedure helps resolve the issue:

1. Separately listen to all sides of the story, including individuals directly involved and any witnesses. Make sure you give each individual space to speak, and avoid interrupting them or speaking over them. Repeat back to them your understanding of what they have said.

2. Ensure the individual(s) involved do not feel like they are being punished. Assure them your interest is the wellbeing of all involved.

3. Always sure everything is documented (especially in the case of a grievance).

4. If there is a discrepancy between what is said or what is entered into the notes be sure to investigate it.

5. Bring the parties together for a solution-focused discussion. If there is a power/hierarchy difference (i.e., Dentist versus Dental Assistant or seasoned versus new staff member) the Dentist/seasoned staff member needs to give space to the assistant/new staff member to voice themselves, otherwise they will come off as disrespectful and undermining.

6. Have both parties problem-solve the incident. If they are unable to come to an agreement, suggest alternatives for them to consider. Once they agree on a resolution and action plan, document the agreement.

7. Use team meetings/staff meetings to problem-solve future instances.

Example

I had a staff member note in the patient file that they had advised the patient over the phone about their upcoming visit, but when the patient came in, it was clear that they had not been informed of some elements of the visit. It happened with a few different people. The individual was relatively new and I did not want them to feel they were being attacked, so I monitored them. Until it was resolved it did create trust issues. I invited the individuals involved to a one-to-one and through the conversation I found out they were lacking confidence. I sat with them on several occasions, coaching them through taking phone calls. I advised them on how to reassure a patient who had not been to the practice in two years; how to review medical history over the phone and update it; how to see if the patient's X-rays were on file or needed updating; whether the patient needed to arrive 15 minutes early for their appointment; and what information the Dentist is looking for on the patient file. When new staff are inducted, or a system changes, they can easily be overwhelmed and may miss a step. Revisiting it together allows you to explain the importance and nuances of why each step is required.

BRIDGING CULTURAL COMMUNICATION ISSUES

Take the time to get to know each staff member (through coffee breaks and lunches) and delve into what it was like for them growing up, and their experiences. Avoid blanket cultural statements (that is, "all Muslims…" or similar). These insights will help you understand why they may respond the way they do when something is going on personally or professionally. One staff member of mine told me how her mother had immigrated from a war-torn country to Australia many years ago and that with COVID-19 and the supermarket scarcity occurring in Australia, her mother felt like she was back in her native birth country again. It was helpful to know that she had these concerns on her mind, which I wouldn't have otherwise known. When you have an understanding of what's going on, you are able to support your staff and anticipate if they may need time to destress.

As a Practice Manager, your role is one of trust, kindness and care, and you offer a judgement-free zone. Know that staff may approach you because they don't know who else to speak with and feel they can trust you. Staff who are not from a Western culture or shifted out of their parents' care (from school to work life) may go through new experiences that they were not permitted to before. For example, women in your practice who may now have the opportunity to go out dancing with friends, date, and experiment with alcohol and drugs. They may feel close to you and wish to share this with you. Use the guidelines and policies of the practice as your boundaries. That is, when discussing recreational drug use, ask whether this is impacting their performance, and advise that they will be monitored.

If not already in place, create an employee manual for all staff that sets out relevant information about the practice, including but not limited to: expectations of staff hours, clocking in/out and conduct; what to do if a staff member is being harassed; annual leave/sick leave (allocated days per year, how much notice is required, any blackout periods and so on); the practice emergency contacts; and the first aid station/officers.

HOW TO BUILD A TEAM OF POWERFUL COMMUNICATORS

USING ROLEPLAY FOR DEVELOPMENT

Using roleplay during staff development days or staff meetings is a great way to explore scenarios that may arise. It provides opportunities for questions staff may have, especially if they have not experienced the scenario playing out. Giving staff complex scenarios and having them work together to come up with a solution helps develop their problem-solving skills as well as building rapport.

BOUNDARIES

The guidelines and policies of the practice state what is expected at all times – everything comes back to these, which sets the boundaries of behaviour.

CHAPTER 5

BUILDING SOFT SKILLS

I have found those who communicate easily tend to create great working relationships, but outside of family and friends, communicating does not come naturally to everyone. Providing a safe and encouraging space within a team will assist those who are quiet, those learning to express their thoughts, or those wishing to ask for help.

Assist in developing a staff member's communication skills simply by delegating a task that they need to update the team about at each meeting. Alternatively, put them in charge of organising the next morning tea. If they start small with a team meeting task, you can then build them up to running a team meeting, and eventually a staff meeting when they feel confident enough.

Listening is another soft skill that is often overlooked. It involves not only hearing what the person is saying, but noticing what their body language is saying as well. At the next staff meeting or team development day, run a session on listening and body language and go through examples of patient/staff interactions as well as staff/staff interactions. In a space where patients in particular are feeling fear or anxiety about their appointment, being able to decode their mood through their words and body language can help us tailor their experience to their needs.

ACTIVITY 14

Soft skills

Make a list of ways you can build soft skills into the workplace.

_____

_____

_____

_____

_____

_____

_____

_____

_____

_____

Are there any boundaries that need to be put in place to make the workplace safer or more comfortable, psychologically and emotionally?

_____

_____

_____

_____

_____

_____

_____

_____

_____

_____

6

GETTING CUSTOMER SERVICE RIGHT EVERY TIME

"Your most unhappy customers are your greatest source of learning."
– Bill Gates

WHO IS YOUR CUSTOMER?

Patients, potential patients and staff are your customers. In terms of staff, their respect for each other and sense of belonging is an indication of the culture of the practice. Encouraging your staff to return day after day, delivering procedures patients are pleased with, and growing the practice, is the result of getting your customer service right every time.

FOUR KEY CHARACTERISTICS REQUIRED IN CUSTOMER CARE

I believe all staff in any dental practice, especially those at the front desk, should embody the following characteristics, whether in person or on the phone: compassion, empathy, respect, equality. I encourage staff to treat everybody the same, whether they are a patient or not. Yes, there will be instances when non-patients will enter the practice who are not there to find out about your services or to make an appointment. The practice should be seen as a safe space in the community, with staff available to help anyone at any time.

Instances when non-patients may enter the practice include:

- Individuals walking in off the street requesting to use a phone to make a call (perhaps if their mobile phone is out of credit). Note: school students may fall into this category as well. One day an individual who was high (on drugs) entered and asked to use the phone; the Front Desk staff were unsure, and on assessing the situation I saw they were very respectful, and allowed them to make the call they needed.

- Individuals who need to use a power point for 15 minutes to charge their phone.

- School students on their way home who have asked to wait in the practice for 15 minutes as they did not feel safe with someone walking behind them.

- Elderly individuals who may need a space to sit for a moment if feeling unwell.

Engaging a Dentist for your mouth health is based on trust, kindness and care factor. The positive experience, trust and kindness received from everyone in the practice, whether they be Front Desk staff, Hygienist or Dentist, is remembered by the individual helped. In future, it may result in a referral or the person you helped choosing to switch Dentists and come to you. That student walking home from school will remember the practice as a place that made them feel comfortable and safe when they are looking for a Dentist or making referrals.

CREATING CUSTOMER SERVICE THAT GOES THE EXTRA MILE

Implementing systems anyone in the practice can follow creates consistency and standards. When the practice I was working in shifted to a holistic health model, I added new processes such as the Discovery Call Screening Sheet and New Patient Exam. Both of these were screenings to ensure the patient was the right fit for the direction of the practice. With the new processes, the Patient Coordinator would ask about the patient's dental anatomy, their previous experience at a dental practice, and if there was anything specific we needed to know. They would then discuss expectations on the day, including payment, because sometimes your particular practice is not what the patient is looking for.

Call screening on new patient enquiries helps quickly identify whether the enquirer is a fit for the practice or not. It could be that they just want the issue fixed and do not care about how the mouth affects their holistic health (that is: bite alignment, missing teeth, decay, being infection-free and so on). Always ask if they have an existing Dentist, if they are after a second opinion, or if they are shopping around for a new Dentist. If the patient is not in pain and not a 'fit' for the practice model, it gives the staff the courage to say that the practice is not the right fit for them and to refer them back to their Dentist. People appreciate honesty, and you never know, further down the track that patient may be looking for something more from a Dentist and return.

Do you have a phone script and new patient screening process in place? If so, are there any changes that it requires?

Entering pop-up notes on a patient's file allows everyone

involved in the patient's care to immediately help put them at ease, and stops the patient from repeating themselves at every visit. For example, a patient may prefer ultrasonic scaling to manual scaling, or a new patient may inform you over the phone that they feel anxious at Dentists.

Follow through on any commitment to patients. If staff advise the patient they will phone or email on a particular date, ensure it happens. This is another touch point where the client feels reassured and valued, and contributes to the consistency and standard of service.

CUSTOMER SERVICE THAT BRINGS A SMILE TO THE PATIENT

To put it simply: always go above and beyond, every time.

Answer the phone with a smile! When a favourite patient comes in, or someone who looks like they need their day brightened, offer them a compliment to bring an instant smile to their face.

During the COVID-19 closure, I sent out an email advising patients that the practice was taking the opportunity to update patient personal contact details and because we had over 5000 people on our database, asked if they would supply a photo to add to their file so we can get to know them better. I received mixed feedback, because some thought it was a scam. However, most patients sent in pictures, and some patients went the extra mile to bring a smile to our day by sending a happy snap taken on overseas travel or with a beer in hand. This is an opportunity to build instant rapport on their next visit as you can comment on or ask a question about the picture. Another tip to stay connected with your patients whenever they email or phone the practice is to thank them. Acknowledge that you have received their information, and that their file has been updated.

When a customer does not feel welcomed or connected to the practice, they become frustrated. You are seen as a 'service' only. Always use eye contact, ask the patient if they understand the information they have been given, and if they have any questions.

Following these guidelines will add to people's first impression of the practice:

- Staff members are to be well groomed (have tidy hair, natural makeup) with clean uniforms.

- Do not make personal phone calls at reception when patients are present in the waiting room.

- No eating of food at the reception desk.

- Breaks are a great way to shift the energy if a staff member needs some time out.

- Glasses and cups should be checked for cleanliness when hand washed or removed from the dishwasher.

- Immediately remove a patient's glass/cup when they are collected for their procedure.

WHAT IMPACTS A PATIENT'S EXPERIENCE?

FEAR

The most common reasons for anxious patients at your practice may be due to:

- Fear of the drill (the sound, smell or feel)

- Fear of pain

- Fear of needles

- The lack of being in control

- A previous bad experience

Train your staff to deal with anxious patients and elevate the experience your practice offers. The care and patience required to help clients relax, and how it contributes to the patient's overall experience, is a team effort. There are many ways you can empower staff to help a patient feel safe, alleviate an element of fear, and help them feel in control:

- Give them a warm welcome and engage them in conversation while they are in the waiting room. This will serve as a great distraction as well as put them at ease.

- Explain each step and ask the patient if there is anything they need before the Hygienist/Dentist begins. For example, they may like a blanket over them, a blanket or tissue to hold, or even for someone to hold their hand.

- Inform the patient how to let you know when they need a break (that is, raise their hand).

- Thoroughly explain any treatment, give them a moment to process what you have told them, and check if they have any questions.

- For lengthy procedures, provide a distraction such as a screen on the ceiling and a choice of a show to watch.

CHAPTER 6

SCENTS

Due to the Dentists, Hygienists and Dental Assistants working in such close proximity to patients, the lack of overpowering body odour is crucial to the comfort of the patient (and colleagues).

Body odour may occur due to:
- Exercising on the way to work (cycling, walking, going to the gym) and changing without showering.

- Overpowering scents (that is, foods the staff member has eaten, such as fish, curries, or from cigarette smoke).

- Overpowering perfumes or deodorants (scents are personal and whether they are obtrusive will vary from person to person).

- Medication may be a contributing factor to changes in the body.

- Hormones.

Ensure staff know they are to wear clean uniforms every day and to arrive well-groomed. Write this in the practice manual. In the event personal hygiene issues arise, do not be afraid to have frank discussion (in private), especially where there are cultural differences. This is an opportunity for them to learn as they adjust to a Western way of life. How do you address it? With care and by remaining neutral.

Begin the conversation with a compliment about their personal grooming. Then follow with, "We work in a clinical environment and part of our position here involves personal grooming. We work closely with other people, and it's important we're mindful of our own body smells and any perfumes/products we're using because they can be offensive to other people."

Use non-confrontational language like, "I have noticed", and state the hygiene matter that has come to your attention. Open a discussion about their personal care routine and ask whether any steps were skipped that may have resulted in the hygiene matter you are discussing. Remember to use caring words.

If hygiene steps were not skipped, discuss how to do it correctly. Provide a demonstration if possible, or offer the individual the personal care item(s) they may be lacking. If they were showering in the evening only but body odour is prominent on arrival at work, suggest showering in the morning before work, or in both the morning and evening.

End the conversation by affirming the person and

assuring them that this hygiene issue does not change your relationship. Help them devise a personal care plan, if appropriate.

Below I have listed common scenarios that cause offensive odours and possible solutions:

- Exercising on the way to work:
    » Getting up earlier to exercise and shower at home before coming to work.
    » If work has a shower on the premises, arrive earlier and take a shower at work.

- Overpowering scents:
    » Do not cook in the uniform.
    » Leave clean uniforms at work to change into on arrival.

- Overpowering perfumes or deodorants:
    » Reducing the amount of deodorant or perfume applied.
    » Instead of spraying directly on the skin or clothing in a concentrated area, spray it up into the air and walking through it so it falls on the clothes lightly.
    » Changing brands.

- Medication:
  - » Revise their medication with their doctor and advise an update.

- Hormonal:
  - » Suggest wipes to freshen up throughout the day.

I suggest you stock the following in your practice:
- Men's and women's deodorant in the change room.

- Feminine hygiene products in the Practice Manager's office for emergencies.

- Shower gel, shampoo and conditioner if there is a shower on the premises.

- Spare uniforms in the event of accidents.

CHAPTER 6

Susie is sharing bonus material.
Visit thedentalconcierge.com.au/book-bonuses

7

BUILDING A HIGH-PERFORMANCE MINDSET IN YOUR TEAM

"The highest levels of performance come to people who are centered, intuitive, creative, and reflective – people who know to see a problem as an opportunity."
– Deepak Chopra

WHAT IS A HIGH-PERFORMANCE MINDSET?

In my experience, I have found the following characteristics of high achievers very beneficial to the practice. High achievers are:

- **Proactive** – proactive in their role, take responsibility for their career progression by requesting and completing training that not only benefits their role but the practice as well, looks at the big picture.

- **Solution-focused** – take the initiative in everything they do, are willing to tweak a process to streamline it further, and look outside the box to find a solution that works for all.

- **Inquisitive** – have a curiosity to question everything and continually learn.

- **Happy, bubbly, energetic, enjoy being at work** – individuals with a cheerful disposition breathe life and energy into the practice (and lift up anxious patients), and colleagues enjoy working with them.

- **Helpful** – are happy to help whenever asked and will follow through on tasks delegated to them; they often go above and beyond.

- **Compassionate** – have the ability to empathise with colleagues in times of distress, know when to give them space to process, and if to assist with a solution-focused path.

- **Task-focused** – remain focused on the task they are participating in and do not get distracted easily.

- Participate in **personal development** outside of the workplace – are interested in bettering themselves, and know the flow-on effects benefit their profession and lead to greater opportunities.

- **Honest** – speaks up when they make a mistake; are willing to voice their opinion if they do not agree and offer alternatives.

- **Respected** and **influential** – an individual who has the trust of their team, is well respected and able to influence others, inspires others to be greater, and contributes to their sense of belonging.

- **Appreciative** – acknowledge the contribution of others, which encourages others to do the same.

BUILDING A HIGH-PERFORMANCE TEAM

You can help extend all staff members to be high-performing individuals and part of a high-performing team by encouraging them to:

- Know their colleagues – Do they have a partner?

What are their interests? And so on.

- Create energy and enthusiasm – enthusiasm is infectious (think of the *When Harry Met Sally* cafe scene). It uplifts everyone and encourages them to be greater.

- Be solution-focused to resolve conflicts and increase cooperation.

- Set s-t-r-e-t-c-h goals and expand individual comfort zones.

- Communicate, communicate, communicate!

- Be trusted and respected by everyone in the practice.

- Reflect and use self-feedback as well as feedback from peers to improve. (Were there any situations that could have been done differently or handled better?)

RESPECTING WHERE STAFF ARE IN THEIR JOURNEY

Although there may be times when you are frustrated

that an individual is not living up to their potential, it is important we respect staff where they are, at that moment. Staff development plans, appraisals and frequent check-ins will help individuals build their confidence in you and the organisation. There may be circumstances that are temporarily holding them back, such as confidence in their own ability, perceived fear, self-imposed limitations or financial concerns. But with encouragement, they can move beyond that. What they choose in the moment, may not be what they choose in a week's or a month's time.

I have offered training to staff with the understanding that the practice would make good use of the new skills they learn. We would also do this in a supportive environment, and they could enhance their learning by putting the skills into practice. Of the five who were interested, I advised that the practice would cover a percentage of the training fee and they would be responsible for the balance of funds. From the five, three chose to proceed, and of those three, two later pulled out. (One was overwhelmed and the second stopped for financial reasons). In the end, out of five, only one ran with the training. Those who did not proceed know what is expected of them if they choose training at a later date. In the meantime, they are able to see the growth of the individual who did complete the training.

WHAT TO LOOK FOR WHEN HIRING STAFF

I invite you to shift the focus of hiring primarily based on skills, knowledge and experience, to one of hiring based on attitude and behaviour. Do they see the cup as half-full or half-empty? Are they determined? What is their level of commitment? Attitude and behaviour are the difference between someone being good and someone being great!

Discuss with the team who the newly hired employee would be working with, in order to outline the role and make sure nothing is missed. Consider technical skills and responsibilities (including infrequent tasks), then go over attitude, characteristics, values, personality fit, and detail these requirements clearly in the job description.

During the interview, give details of the role, discuss the culture of the team and organisation – individuals are looking for more than job security. The applicant can see exactly what is required for the role (and the detail may help weed out those who are not a good fit). Invite questions during the interview stage from both parties – the applicant can get clarity, and the practice can dig deeper into their experience. It also provides a guide about performance (whether it will be above or below expectations).

We have all experienced great hires and poor hires.

CHAPTER 7

Avoid getting caught up in their enthusiasm and hype in the interview, and neglecting all questions on your checklist. I have been there. I once had an individual who presented as the ideal candidate in their interview, said everything I needed to hear and ticked all the boxes. Once they commenced at the practice, however, they didn't deliver.

Reflecting on each hiring experience, I updated the hire process to include the following components:

Getting to know the individual and ask about:
- Their previous career experience (not just the position they are in currently in).

- What their values are.

- What do they like to do in their downtime (sport, hobbies, personal development, volunteering, and so on).

- Their current role – ask them about their current team and get them to give you an example of when the team has pulled together, and when it became fractured.

Explaining about our practice:
- The practice operating model, including hours, culture, and so on.

- Values of the practice.

- How they should show up to work (personal grooming).

- Reiterate the importance of personal grooming.

Discussing the role and responsibilities:
- What is required in the role and who they will be working with, team dynamics, and so on.

- What they are looking for in this role and from the practice.

- What their desired career trajectory is.

Testing:
- List scenarios that play out in the clinic and ask how they would handle the situation.

- Ask questions that give you an indication of their attitude.

- Literacy test – entering the correct information into the practice software is essential.

- For administration staff I include numeracy tests (calculating a 5% and 10% discount).

KEY QUALITIES TO LOOK FOR WHEN HIRING A PRACTICE MANAGER

A Practice Manager is someone who can step into all roles of the clinic. They are a:

Calm and diplomatic operator:
- Are friendly, composed, outgoing, approachable

- Can deal with HR to problem-solve team issues and customer complaints

- Have excellent communication skills

- Can deal with pressure

Team leader:
- Have gratitude and appreciation for their team

- Are able to receive and give constructive feedback

- Are team-oriented and able to boost team morale

- Work alongside team, not behind them or behind closed doors

- Are proactive in demonstrating leadership and developing individuals

- Have confidence and performance in managing and appraising the team

- Can demonstrate the line between their job role and the team

Professional:
- Rarely takes unscheduled time off

- Are presentable

- Show professionalism

- Are well-organised and have a business mindset

- Practise the dental clinic values

- Follow fair work guidelines

Multi-skilled:
- Are adept at IT systems, Governance, clinic maintenance, marketing

- Are responsible for financials of the clinic

KEY QUALITIES TO LOOK FOR WHEN HIRING ADMINISTRATION STAFF

Your administration employees are the first people your clients will interact with; therefore, it is important that they make a good impression. They are a:

People person:
- Are warm and welcoming

- Show empathy and compassion

- Are friendly and charismatic but have an assertive approach

- Deliver exceptional customer service

- Are able to coordinate with diverse people

- Are reassuring to clients, particularly those who are about to undergo a dental procedure

Professional:
- Are able to maintain relationships with all employees

- Are able to work independently

- Are presentable and keep the administration area neat and tidy

- Take the job seriously and not personally

- Are able to use their initiative and deal with pressure

- Can deal with HR to problem-solve team issues and customer complaints

- Are able to use clear language and have great interpersonal skills

Organised:
- Have excellent organisational and time management skills

- Are able to multitask and perform different administration duties daily

- Have sound appointment book understanding (can colour code and categorise the dental procedure and use pre blocks according to clinic needs)

Multi-skilled:
- Have excellent literacy and numeracy skills

- Are able to answer ALL phone calls, emails, SMS; acknowledge all clients attending the practice

- Have an understanding of all dental procedures

- Are able to make notes and follow dental guidelines, ensuring patient files are up to date at check in or on the phone

- Undertake all weekly and monthly tasks

KEY QUALITIES TO LOOK FOR WHEN HIRING A DENTAL ASSISTANT

When hiring a Dental Assistant, you will need to decide if it will be a position for a trainee (newbie) or a Dental Assistant with a qualification. Most dental clinics will accept a Dental Assistant with a Certificate III in Dental Assisting. These days, some practices may require

Certificate IV in Dental Assisting with Radiology Certificate and Oral Health Therapy. High quality Dental Assistants have:

Motivation and flexibility:
- Are open to being mentored and go the extra mile to perform better

- Use their initiative and allow themselves to become part of the team rather than have an 'I know everything' attitude

- Use their experience as leverage and shift their thinking, from thinking that they are not significant to a more positive attitude

- Allow themselves to be become part of the workplace and make the most of their skillset (that is, if they can use a triplex water gun to its full capacity, and so forth)

- Can balance duties effortlessly

- Can be flexible

CHAPTER 7

Interpersonal skills:
- Have great communication skills

- Demonstrate exceptional customer service

- Are able to maintain relationships with all employees

- Are able to understand the patient and get to know them

Dental knowledge:
- Have an understanding of all dental procedures and learn how the Dentist operates

- Have dental procedure knowledge and understand instrument/equipment setup

- Are able to use analogies based on a patient's personal notes such as likes and interests, and We Know Yous (WKYs)

Attention to detail:
- Demonstrate excellent infection control

- Have excellent organisational and time management skills

- Read and look across the appointment book in order to decipher the next steps of the Dentist, the other dental room operating and the whole clinic

Consider trialling shortlisted applicants on work or non-workday(s), remunerating them for their time. It is a perfect opportunity to see firsthand their interaction with the team, their technical and soft skills. If it's a non-workday, practice staff can act as dummy patients with differing scenarios to see how they perform, and the team can discuss their thoughts afterwards. If they were to trial with clients, a client confidentiality form would need to be signed. For the shortlisted application, they have a true insight into the practice and can make an informed decision whether the role is for them or not.

HOW TO FOSTER A HIGH PERFORMER

There will always be individuals seeking to specialise beyond what your practice offers. However, for most, with career planning, goal setting (and achieving), training and opportunities to develop their soft and hard skills, your high performers will bloom and choose to remain with you for many years.

CHAPTER 7

I have found a combination of the following fosters loyalty amongst high performers:

- Have the high performer contribute to growing the organisation and team culture, team dynamics and job enjoyment by seeking their input.

- Set key performance indicators (KPIs) for the high performer, encouraging them to contribute to the growth of the practice (that is, revenue, services, patients) and link to a bonus payment. Review these on a weekly or monthly basis.

- Have the high performer lead others. They can develop their leadership and communication skills through mentoring, training, and leading meetings. Place the high performer with individuals whom they may not 'gel' with easily and help build their soft skills.

- Ensure they are receiving mentoring from their supervisor (hard and soft skills) and Practice Manager (soft skills) and have them practise these skills as situations arise. Stretch their comfort zone.

- Trust and believe. Always have the high performer's back when they are within the guidelines in order to demonstrate unity to staff. Give them recognition.

- For going above and beyond, surprise and delight high performers in their language, whether that be verbal acknowledgement at staff meetings, gift vouchers/movie tickets, flowers/food, or acts of service (giving them a paid day off) and so on.

- Financially reward them. For example, you could increase their hourly rate, offer additional hours, pay for their parking (if not included), pay for training, and/or send them to industry events.

DEALING WITH PRESSURE

High performers have difficult moments, just like the rest of us, whether it is internal pressure to perform, or external pressures, such as dealing with anxieties from staff and patients, or disagreements with colleagues. At staff meetings, regularly reiterate the culture of 'talking up, not down'. This means talking to your supervisor and finding solutions, not down to your colleagues, and to utilise the Practice Manager to help them shift the situation.

Whenever you see someone under pressure (whether staff or patient), connect with them to see how they are doing and ask if there is anything you can assist them with.

CHAPTER 7

Pressure reception/administration staff may experience

Scenario	Appropriate response Use proactive, positive and helpful language
Unable to accommodate a particular appointment at short notice	Unfortunately, the earliest I can fit you in is <date>. Would you like to be placed on our waitlist in the event an opening becomes available?
Dealing with a demanding, aggressive or inappropriately cheeky individual when they are making an appointment on the phone	Demanding – I'll do my best to help. Tell me what the problem is, and if I can't work something out over the phone, I will give you a call back (then proceed to make the appointment). Aggressive – I understand your need to see <name>. Please be patient and refrain from using that tone, I'm doing my best to help you. The earliest I can fit you in is <date>. (If they don't calm down, ask them to call you back.) Cheeky – <Name> would you please refrain from making those comments, let's keep the conversation professional, otherwise I will be hanging up the phone.

Financial conversations concerning payments that are overdue	In person – take the patient to a section of the desk where there is more privacy or to a client room to discuss payment options (such as a payment plan). Over phone – discuss payment options and ensure the outcome is agreed upon with first payment taken over the phone (where possible).
Mistake by the practice – when they have sent out a late payment notice when customer advises bill has been paid	I'm sorry \<name\>, it's not recorded on our system. Let's work this out, what date did you pay and I'll check the statements.
Complaints	I'm sorry to hear that \<name\>. Let me forward your call to the Practice Manager and they'll be able to help you.
High volume of calls	Ask another administration staff member for assistance or the Practice Manager until the calls settle down.

CHAPTER 7

Pressure from a client whilst in treatment due to anxiety

Patient anxieties are exacerbated when dental staff fail to ask the patient questions or listen to their response and act accordingly. If the Dentist team is not paying attention, they are likely to make a mistake, which affects their energy and demeanour. This can also increase the patient's anxiety, outcome and chance of returning. When staff notice a patient has been triggered (they might exhibit a pale skin tone, excessive sweating, tears or signs of panic), stop the procedure and find out what is going on for the patient. Listen, remain calm and quiet (if required). Ask the following questions:

- Would you like to sit up? (Automatically get them a tissue and a cup of water.)

- Are you in pain?

- Has something triggered you? Is it the adrenaline? (Have a chat with them to identify what triggered them.)

- Would you like me to hold your hand, or would you like to hold a tissue or blanket?

- Would you like a blanket over you to feel snug?

> (Sometimes a blanket is enough to make them feel calm.)

- Reassure them you are there for them, and to speak up if they need anything.

Have the Dental Assistant remain in the room with the patient if they need some time to compose themselves. This will help reassure them. If inexperienced with patient anxiety, the staff member may take a patient's anxiety personally, and if they fail to shift the incident (go for a walk, talk to a supervisor) they are likely to stay in the drama.

MANAGING STAFF UNDER PRESSURE

If they are in the middle of a procedure and it is evident the staff member needs to be removed from the situation, substitute in another colleague who will help alleviate the pressure. If not, when they are finished with the patient, suggest they take themselves out of the practice and change the scene by going for a walk, grabbing a coffee, sitting outdoors in the sun and breathing. If you can get them to laugh at a bad joke, laughter will help shift their mindset quicker than anything else.

Following the incident, have a discussion with the staff member about dealing with pressure, and offer them options, such as: speaking up to their supervisor, Practice Manager or trusted staff member; self-reflecting at the end of the day through asking, "How could I have made the situation different?"; and listing ways they can self-evaluate and make changes during the procedure in future occurrences. Do they need further training? What made them uncomfortable or succumb to pressure? The more they tap into their awareness and recognise it in the future, the quicker they can change the situation.

DUTY OF CARE

During a treatment at one of the practices I worked at, a Dentist felt the assistant was not present and struggled in the procedure. The Dentist lacked support and had to ask for everything they needed. The procedure was paused, the assistant removed mid-treatment, and the roster reshuffled. Taking the assistant aside, I asked if there was something going on I needed to know about. I followed this up with asking whether they wanted to be at work that day. When asking this question, I reassured them that it was okay if they did not wish to be there. They could go home and would still be paid. I stressed that if they wished to remain at work, they had to change their performance. I emphasised their duty of care not only to the patient, but to their colleagues and themselves, so they did not end up injured. If they did not wish to

ACTIVITY 15

Reflecting on incidents

- Was it handled appropriately?

  _____

  _____

- Could it have been handled differently or better?

  _____

  _____

- What could the practice put in place to create better solutions?

  _____

  _____

  _____

  _____

be at work, I would ask them why they chose to come to work that day. Their response indicates what they are driven by. Some individuals have some much going on in their personal life, but they have run out of personal or annual leave and feel forced to come to work because they need the money. Bringing it back to the duty of care keeps their performance within the guidelines and is not seen as a punishment. Not performing creates extra pressure on the workplace and mistakes can happen. If they choose to come to work, then their attitude and focus must be 'on' when they walk in the door. If they choose not to be at work, a phone call first thing in the morning allows the book to be shuffled. It is making it safer, more pleasant and productive for all involved.

ADDITIONAL SUPPORT

If a staff member appears to be under pressure for an extended period of time (i.e., for weeks) and their needs are beyond your capacity, remind them the Employee Assistance Program (EAP) is available, where they can seek counselling sessions to talk to someone outside of the practice. It is confidential and they receive free sessions.

Asking them if they need to take an extended leave of absence (paid or unpaid depending on their leave balances), allows them to make a decision knowing their job is secure.

8

SOLVE THESE 9 PROBLEMS AND YOU WILL BE AHEAD OF THE GAME

"You've got to stay ahead of the game to be able to stay in it."
– **Kate Moss**

The Practice Manager's role includes having a bird's-eye view of the practice, identifying any areas of disharmony, and rectifying them to ensure a consistent balance.

PROBLEM 1: CONSISTENCY

Consistency of service is delivered when the practice is streamlined and running like a well-oiled machine. It occurs when everybody is aligned, proficient in what they are doing and generating favourable results. Consistency sets the rhythm of the day and has the ability to flex with ease, if the rhythm suddenly changes.

Consistency should be visible across these elements of the practice:

- Staff presentation – uniform, personal grooming, smile, tone of voice.

- Environment – welcoming, calm and tidy, replenished consumables.

- Language – open and supportive.

- Patient journey – making appointments, updating patient files, treatment, ease of financial transaction, positive feedback.

CHAPTER 8

- Staff actions – understanding and knowledge of the practice policies and guidelines, fluency in procedure steps and anticipation of the next steps.

Consistency can easily be disrupted when:

- New staff members are getting to know the practice guidelines and systems.

- Personal situations disrupt the workspace (for example, staff who have current personal issues appear stressed, anxious or distracted, may snap at others, may get upset easily, and their level of service slips, such as missing or forgetting steps).

- Individuals start doing their own thing instead of adhering to practice guidelines and systems.

- A system is no longer efficient and takes more time than in the past.

- Staff lack confidence in the information recorded in the file or what they were told, and extra time is required to check the information.

- Staff disputes require additional resources such as mediation.

ACTIVITY 16

Consistency Audit

- Are there any areas of the practice you can identify that lack consistency?

  _____

  _____

  _____

  _____

- What can be instituted to ensure consistency?

  _____

  _____

  _____

  _____

  _____

CHAPTER 8

PROBLEM 2: COMPLETING TASKS

There are the odd occasions where non-essential daily tasks are not completed due to an overwhelm on resources, and can be shifted to the next day. But if this occurs frequently, then the abilities of staff or the system need to be reviewed. Essential daily tasks may include opening up the practice, checking the SMS system is working, making reminder calls, daily backups, accounts pre-settlement and settlement, closing the practice down for the day, cleaning (emptying trash bins, putting on dishwasher, and so on), and setting the rooms up for the first appointment the following day.

When individuals, teams or systems are new, the gaps in completing tasks I have noted usually relate to a lack of confidence (for example: the fear of doing the task incorrectly, looking stupid in front of their colleagues, getting into trouble, not knowing how to approach one another, and so on). A team cannot have each other's back if they don't know what is going on. Then, frustration begins to dismantle the harmony of the team. Reiterate to staff that speaking up when you need assistance is crucial for additional support, whether this is just an ad hoc task due to short staffing, whether extra training is required, or if changes to the current system need to be made. Speaking up demonstrates being proactive. Give staff tips. If they are not sure how to approach an individual, tell them to have a chat with the other person and ask them how they would like to be approached. Above all, keep it simple.

If you feel a staff member is not speaking up, getting overwhelmed and repeatedly fails to complete tasks, you need to look at whether they are in the right role for their abilities. A conversation about the job role requirements, their time management and performance, and their job satisfaction will also help them identify whether the role is right for them. You can discuss the possibility of shifting them into another role within the practice (if available), or whether they leave and seek that role elsewhere.

I remember an administrative staff member who was new to the dental industry, and the reception role they were in was not working for them. I switched them to the clinical department for six months (which they loved) and immersed them in all clinical aspects, including sterilisation procedures, terminology, and how the practice worked. There were occasions when I needed to switch them back to reception temporarily and the difference in the ability and confidence was remarkable – they understood the different treatments, what was required for each appointment, and could translate that to the patient.

CHAPTER 8

PROBLEM 3: TIME MANAGEMENT

Daily planning and monitoring the appointment book ('bible') is essential. Time can be saved during treatments when the correct equipment is set up prior to the patient taking the chair. There will always be changes to best laid plans, and regular updates enable instantaneous changes when needed. This may be in the form of a three- to five-minute group huddle or simply advising patients of appointment time delays or reschedules (due to emergencies, for example).

During COVID-19, when updated guidelines from the Australian Dental Association were regularly rolled out, we updated processes to include any additional time. We contacted patients with bookings and reassured them if they were not comfortable coming to the practice, we understood, and if they woke up unwell, not to put the practice or themselves at risk. We increased patient screening processes. For staff, we updated personal protective equipment continually, and if staff were mid-treatment, we sought the patient's permission to update the staff member. Patients are appreciative when kept informed rather than left wondering why they have been left alone in the room.

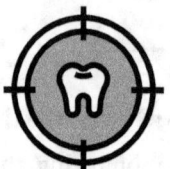

PROBLEM 4: EFFICIENCY

Task completion, time management and consistency equally contribute to the efficiency of the team and practice.

Efficiency is the result of confidence, future planning and being organised. And there is efficiency from individuals and from teams. Need to get a team moving more efficiently? Focus on the team leader to engage, guide and energise their team.

PROBLEM 5: ATTITUDE

I believe if you have a positive, driven attitude, you can accomplish anything. You enjoy and thrive at your workplace.

If you have got a 'Negative Nellie' whose glass is always half-empty, what they do achieve will be seen as a struggle. They will do what is required, nothing more without being asked, and their job satisfaction will be average.

I have also experienced the social butterfly, who loved interacting but proved to be more of an interrupter of other people's time. At first, they lacked confidence so I paired them up with two buddies, but the butterfly lacked awareness that the others also needed to complete their job. The butterfly was focused on their own needs, ignored the practice policies, and their personal life drama frequently seeped into the practice. They needed their performance managed and boundaries set. A frank discussion around what the practice requires, their performance and whether the job was a good fit for them helps them realise this job may not be for them.

PROBLEM 6: COMMUNICATION

Spoken communication in the practice needs to be backed up with written communication, as the practice relies heavily on the accuracy of the appointment book and client files. And the information must be clear.

Common communication issues that occur between administration staff and clinical staff include:

- Neglecting the appointment book – it is the heart of the workplace, a living and breathing component of the dental ecosystem. It needs to be updated constantly with patient movement as they progress between practitioners, treatments and rooms, and in accordance with health and safety guidelines. It is essential to know where patients are at all times in the event of an emergency or evacuation.

- Documentation gaps – if medical history is not preempted, collected over the phone and entered into the system, it can result in frustration and duplication of time.

- New staff are still building their understanding of how the practice and its systems work.

Communicate, communicate, communicate. Use roleplay in group meetings or training to address communication lapses, tapping into the different learning styles of everyone present. Demonstrate scenarios that arise and have them problem-solve together so staff truly understand the impact a misstep creates. When it comes to new staff, a visual demonstration of each treatment helps them understand and translate what will take place for the patient, and they will know what to enter into the system for appointments.

Communication issues that can arise between patients and administration staff:
- Not understanding how the practice operates (that is, time required for treatment, deposit paid for treatment, and so on).

- Consistency of care on arrival, in the waiting room and on account settlement.

I always promote that you need to inform and educate patients. Explain what the process is, what the practice will deliver and what is expected of them. They have a need to understand and feel cared for. We get to demonstrate that they are not just a number when they come to this practice. The patient wants to know when spending money at the practice that they are getting the value they perceive.

Consistency of service and care is important. People are

creatures of habit. A patient comes in every six months, they may sit in the same chair, and sometimes they come early so they can have a coffee to take a breather from their busy day. If you do not give them that coffee, that one time, they will make sure they tell you about it. Adding notes and idiosyncrasies to the patient file helps new staff get to know everyone who visits the practice. They will discover the patient has been coming to the practice for 20 years and can automatically ask them if they would like their coffee of choice.

I recently had a patient who came from another practice because the practice could not do the procedure that was required. Afterwards we were chatting, and I asked for feedback on the service they received. They responded that they had been taking notes about what we do to implement in their own legal business. It was great to hear a business owner's point of view and I thanked them. When you work day in, day out on the other side of the business, you do not always see the patient experience. It reinforced the importance of policies and processes because when staff get busy (and sometimes overwhelmed), they have the processes to fall back on and the level of service remains consistent. To this day, I still refer to the policies and guidelines.

CHAPTER 8

PROBLEM 7: RELATIONSHIP CONFLICTS

In today's cultural and generational mix, no matter how sound your organisation is, individuals working closely together can quickly move from a simple misunderstanding or disagreement to a conflict that affects the workplace.

Embrace diversity – encourage discussions around ethnicities, genders, ages, religions, disabilities, and sexual orientations over a Bring-a-Plate shared lunch. Examples include:

- **Cultural and religious events** – Chinese New Year, Harmony Day, Greek Easter, end of Ramadan, Bastille Day, Oktoberfest, Remembrance Day, Hanukkah. You can celebrate the cultural events of the nationalities of the practice staff.

- **Diversity events** – International Women's Day, Close the Gap Day, National Sorry Day, Wear It Purple Day, Equal Pay Day, International Men's Day, White Ribbon Day (to raise awareness about violence against women). Why not shift

International Women's Day and International Men's Day to an inclusion day and recognise individual contributions (male or female) to the organisation? Staff could nominate another staff member who has gone above and beyond in their eyes (for example, through mentoring staff, always helping out, regularly checking in with staff who are unwell, and so on).

- **Disability and mental health events** – R U Ok? Day, International Day of Persons with Disabilities.

Staff members who get along well and are always together (including during breaks) risk excluding others. Encourage them to include other team members in their break time conversations if they are sitting in a communal space. Encourage them to get to know their colleagues, what they are great at in the workplace, as well as what they do in their personal time.

When it comes to individual beliefs, simply agree to disagree and respect the others' beliefs. Where there has been a conflict and we have worked or are working through it, I get the individuals involved to put their differences aside and complete a task where they need to communicate and work together. It can be anything from:

- Baking a cake together for the next birthday or staff luncheon.

- Pairing them together for a team-building exercise.

Have individuals create their own boundaries and clearly voice to others if they are crossing it. Ultimately if they cannot resolve the issue and be respectful to each other in the workplace, it impacts their enjoyment and one will end up leaving, whether or not it is of their choosing.

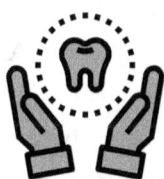

PROBLEM 8: EXPECTATIONS

The role of the practice is to manage the patient's expectations: to dig deep to fully understand what it is they want. We have had patients come in with a photo of what they would like, expecting to be able to get the same 'look' for their teeth. However, the look cannot be met without extensive treatment because of their dental anatomy. We have to clearly and honestly advise alternative options, be mindful of the patient's budget and encourage them to seek a second opinion because we do not want them to make a decision based on hope. Some of our past incidents have given us our biggest learnings.

We had a scenario where the patient wanted porcelain white teeth, which we were able to do. Unfortunately, in the end, it was a case of the patient and Dentist not clearly communicating with each other. The patient did not put forward that they wanted the 'flat, even' look of their white teeth. Their natural dental anatomy was not flat or even because of the way they had ground their teeth. The procedure became extensive as we rebuilt their bite, and there was a significant cost to the practice (chair time, additional lab fees) for redoing parts of their procedure. The priority of the practice was a satisfied patient. Afterwards we reviewed the incident to capture greater clarity for the future.

The next scenario came from one of our long-term patients advocating our practice. We completed veneers on this patient and they looked great. They naturally had a perfect bite so little additional work was required. We received an inquiry from an individual who had seen the referral's results and requested the same. After consultation (they had a midline misalignment) the individual was happy to proceed with the procedure and paid cash up front. While the Dentist was constructing the teeth, we discovered they were *very* anxious in the chair, and due to a lab error and ill fit, one of the teeth split on removal and they freaked out mid-treatment. In the patient's eyes they had instantly lost confidence in the Dentist's abilities. They demanded their money back, and when in my office, tried standover tactics and threats to get a refund. I stood up, even though I was trembling inside, and asked them to stop speaking to me in that manner. I said that they would receive their money on a particular date and time, it must be collected by them, and that they would not be receiving a full refund because they were happy with the treatment that had already been completed prior to that day. On receipt of the refund, I requested they not return because of their expectations. Unfortunately, they had not shopped around for a second opinion before starting treatment. I remember the Practice Principal asking me if I was sure I wanted to take on this case, and I had said yes because we do not judge anybody. However, I failed to heed the warning my intuition had been telling me.

PROBLEM 9: PRACTICE MANAGER LEAVE PLANNING

To ease the anxiety of the organisation when the Practice Manager takes an extended period of leave or leaves the organisation altogether, planning is essential for a smooth transition.

If you need to recruit for the role due to extended leave, such as long service leave, maternity leave or personal leave, then allow ample time to find the 'right fit'. If your replacement can shadow you and take over before your departure, this will give you the opportunity to impart any nuances in the practice.

For a handover allow:
- Existing staff member – one week (or more depending on their skill level)

- New employee filling role – two weeks

When it comes to shorter leave periods, that is, one to two weeks personal leave, the role can easily be broken down and allocated to staff. Consider who is trained, who would appreciate the opportunity to learn a new skill, and who is willing to take on extra responsibilities during the leave period. If we break down the tasks, consider who has the knowledge to handle:
- Payroll and banking

- Human resources

- Social media posting

- Point of contact for the alarm system, and so on

Discuss your suggestion(s) with the Practice Principal, then ask the staff member if they are confident and willing to take on the additional tasks. Give them a choice.

With regards to any people's issues, can this be escalated to the Practice Principal? Can payroll be automated and reconciled on your return (that is: sick leave, annual leave that occurs in your absence)?

Most importantly: if you are the Practice Manager, make sure you unplug from the practice when you are on leave – switch off, enjoy quality time with friends and family. If something cannot be resolved, the Practice Principal will step in. If all else fails, they will call you.

Do you have a contingency Practice Manager Leave Plan ready to go in the event of an unexpected extended absence of leave?

Scan the QR code to download these 9 problems.

9

POSITIVE SELF-MANAGEMENT AND TEAM MANAGEMENT

"Success is not the key to happiness. Happiness is the key to success. If you love what you are doing, you will be successful."
– Albert Schweitzer

A health focus and positive mindset should be at the forefront of wellbeing in any practice, and include the 'small' things that make a difference. I get staff to think about their health through:

- Ensuring there is always food in the cupboard that they can snack on – fruit, muesli bars and other healthy snacks.

- Reminding staff to drink water. The practice installed an alkaline filter tap for staff.

- Checking in with individuals that they have taken their break, because there are some staff who will just keep working unless asked. Keep an eye on the Front Desk staff where time can slip by when they are busy with calls and patients.

- Reminding staff to check in on each other as well, which is also a perfect opportunity to get to know other staff members.

- Giving little health tips that I include in my day. I suggest that they go outside and look at the blue sky, or grab a coffee and go for a 10-minute walk.

- Checking in when someone's having a bad day. I take the time to make them smile (even for a moment) to help shift them out of it.

The workplace culture focuses on having a healthy balance in life. When asked (and relevant), I do share my personal experiences. I have many staff who come to me seeking guidance, whether it is a staff issue or a health issue. If they are not feeling good, it is easy to check in with them to find out if they are eating well, exercising and getting enough sleep. This helps them see where they are at and what they can adjust to feel better.

CHAPTER 9

I discovered that since changing operations and returning to a four-day week, we have reduced high volume stress in the workplace. This shift creates less volume in traffic, the staff members do not feel rushed, and it helps avoid WHS injuries, (for example, there is a decrease in sharps injuries, which can happen when under pressure). There is enough time allocated so the staff are able to close down. During COVID-19, I updated the guidelines to work around the new infection control, including daily cleaners. Surprisingly, this was another win for the staff. Never underestimate how excited your team can be with small changes.

I always encourage personal development courses (along with professional development courses) to keep the mind active. I feel that if you are not willing to work on creating greater things in your personal life, you are not willing to work on your professional self. In 2019, some staff chose to join me for the Tony Robbins event in Sydney, and they loved it. It was amazing to see them in the months afterwards as they made changes in their personal and professional lives. They were happier and their work relationships and levels of trust improved. For 2020, the practice purchased everyone's tickets to go to Tony Robbins in Sydney. Staff were to pay for their own flights and accommodation. We made the decision to pay for staff tickets so they would have exposure to and could experience a growth mindset. It is always different hearing about mindset from someone who is not in the workplace as you can connect on a more personal level.

We have open discussions at work over lunchtime. When it is a team luncheon, we close the practice for that hour to make sure everyone's involved. We leave a note on the door to let patients know that we are breaking for lunch. On occasion, we get out of the practice altogether and head to the local RSL. At other times, staff will bring their runners to work and we will all go for a walk. I like to change the environment, like shifting the morning huddle from the break room to the carpark outside. And sometimes I pretend I am Richard Simmons in lycra (remember the 80s?) and get everyone stretching. Naturally, they think I am crazy, but it makes them smile, gets their blood pumping and strengthens the culture of the workplace. I make sure I mention these activities when interviewing potential new staff to set expectations, and if they are not interested in joining in, they can make the choice that works for them before accepting a position. It helps filter out any individuals who are not a culture fit.

CHAPTER 9

Make a list of courses or personal training workshops you can attend to grow yourself and your team.

_____

_____

_____

_____

_____

_____

_____

_____

_____

_____

_____

_____

_____

10

LEADERSHIP & DIRECTION – THE ART OF MOVING YOUR SUPPORT TEAM FORWARD

> *"Leadership is the capacity to translate vision into reality."*
> – **Warren Bennis**

ESSENTIAL TRAITS OF LEADING

Whatever the position – Front Desk staff, Dental Assistants, the Practice Manager, Hygiene Coordinator, Practice Principal – they are all leadership roles, and in any leadership role, experience, initiative and confidence are necessities. Significant experience in the industry and role hone the hard and soft skills of the individual, as well as confidence. Initiative involves thinking outside the box and changing immediately where necessary, to be proactive rather than reactive. Confidence is threefold: it is the individual's ability in themselves to lead a team; it is the confidence of the team in its leader to be led; and it is confidence that the team can carry out the tasks required for their role. While experience remains with an individual, confidence can strengthen, falter or be lost, based on belief, ability and attitude.

To lead, you need to have clear communication and be adaptable within a structure. When you have an emergency situation, you have got to be able to think and take action within those guidelines. Contingencies need to be planned for, and processes identified and listed to put into action. This is in order to shift the practice from chaos towards its rhythm of harmony. The leader needs to determine how it will affect the workplace before making any decision, and then communicate it to all involved. Even though there is the desire to help the patient, the operational side needs to be considered, as does the eventuality of running past closing time.

Here is an example of leadership falling down. During COVID-19, elderly patients were advised not to have appointments with the Dentist. This was to help keep their exposure to the virus at a minimum due to their increased

CHAPTER 10

risk. One of our existing patients in her 80s walked in, in pain. After talking with the patient, the front desk member spoke with the Practice Principal who made the decision to see the patient. The day fell into chaos as the change in the appointment book was not communicated. This impacted operations and by the time the team knew what was going on they were already running behind. The domino effect was that appointments ran 30 minutes late, patients were waiting longer than necessary, the clinical department ran behind, sanitising rooms was difficult as the room rotation timings were out, the day ended later than normal, and staff were bitching about why the front desk accepted the walk-in. The Practice Principal did reassure the Front Desk staff member that they made the right decision in their duty of care.

What should have happened was that once the Dentist determined how long the treatment would take, the Dental Assistant needed to communicate this to the front desk and the front desk team needed to review and update the book. They should have had the opportunity to identify which patients could be possibly shifted, and phone patients booked in that day to let them know of the delay. If the 30-minute delay did not work for the patient, they could have been rebooked for another day, and then they could have moved appointments forward if someone rescheduled. That would have reorganised the appointment book, which should then have been communicated to team leaders to advise the changes to their teams. There would have been no need for people to question the decision to see the walk-in. In this case, on the following day we commenced with a discussion of what had happened and what could be taken from the experience to improve future occurrences.

LEADERSHIP TRAITS BY ROLE

Each person in the practice can benefit from leadership training, no matter which role they undertake.

Front Desk team

Their leadership begins with communication and clarity: capturing and relaying information, embodying warmth and being welcoming, courteous and polite, and having certainty in directing the flow of the practice. They need the ability to focus and organise as they deal with the pressure of noise around them – calls, patients checking in/checking out and so forth.

Clinical support team

The clinical support team, just like the front desk team, needs to have clear communication skills. Their level of pressure is greater when clients experience anxiety, and their level of nurturing is greater than any other team when supporting the patient. Mental and physical agility is important to switch between patient treatments, including mid-treatment.

Practice Manager

This is a superstar who has the ability to have a bird's-eye view of the practice and be aware of the moving components. They can multitask, have an ability to forecast, problem-solve, delegate and own their decisions because, at the end of the day, they are the final decision maker, and open to feedback. The Practice Manager needs to set relationship boundaries so that they are not taken advantage of. It is important that the Practice Manager is emotionally strong and empathetic but also decisive, streetwise, and firm for tough conversations (for example, if staff are late to work, abuse their sick leave, are under the influence because of recreational drug use and so on).

As the appointment book creates the flow of the practice, the Practice Manager should schedule downtime to allow the front desk team to complete certain tasks, otherwise operations become affected, which impacts staff health and wellbeing. Staff can become overwhelmed in times of high volume when they do not have time to breathe or a moment to catch up.

I schedule the year's big events in advance at the beginning of the year. I then schedule the events for the upcoming quarter, in the first month of that quarter. I schedule the month in the first week of the month. I structure what happens weekly before the first day of the week. This structure works side by side with the appointment book.

I work very closely with the Practice Principal and the Clinical Coordinator. It is important to have a strong working relationship and to build a support system for yourself with colleagues you can bounce ideas off.

HOW GREAT LEADERSHIP GIVES GOOD DIRECTION

A great leader is able to assess the situation, make the judgement call and be confident with the decision they made when communicating to their team. How do you prepare your team members to be leaders? Both training and roleplaying scenarios teach them to have that bird's-eye view of the practice and how each role is impacted in incidents.

Everybody can lead in their daily life within their role. Notice when a process has fallen over due to human error. What can you do to get it back on track within the guidelines, whether it was your error or not? Human error occurs when there is missing information, miscommunication or failure to follow the process. If you see that a system needs improvement, for example, an issue that staff regularly question you about or discuss repeatedly amongst themselves, rather than you solving it as the Practice Manager, bring it up at a meeting and have the staff discuss the problem and come up with solutions. You may need to facilitate the conversation if there are members who are more reserved than others. Once the process is agreed upon, test it and discuss it with other teams before implementing.

Your role is to help others develop their leadership skills as they progress towards their career goals. When you micromanage, you erode confidence. You can reach a goal in many different ways. Everyone's brain functions differently. Remind them the outcome is to reach the goal, and give them the opportunity to achieve it in their way. This means that they will take ownership of the issue and solution. Likewise, avoid micromanaging the administration team. Allow them to make mistakes, set boundaries for them to analyse, have them test and measure to find a solution, and then communicate it to you. It gives them the space to grow and obtain knowledge. It is one thing to 'know' what needs to be done, but it's another to spend time trying, failing, trying again and succeeding to build the soft skills required for leadership.

Great leaders need to look after themselves better physically and mentally, so they have the sharpness of mind to adapt and the energy to implement.

SKYROCKET YOUR LEADERSHIP SKILLS

If you desire to be the best you can be and grow exponentially – not only in your own growth, but your career and the growth of the practice – I highly recommend doing personal development work. My mother is my inspiration, she always waved her fist and told me that I have to be strong! My mentors inspired me and introduced me to Tony Robbins' work.

I recommend to any Practice Manager to invest in their professional development by taking a course in Neuro-Linguistic Programming (NLP). NLP is "the practice of understanding how people organise their thinking, feeling, language and behaviour to produce the results they do."[6] NLP provides tools for improving performance in areas such as communication, management, education, training and counselling. With these tools, you are able to identify the beliefs and patterns staff may be stuck in, and know what will help them change their thoughts and actions, if they choose to change.

CHAPTER 10

WHY LEADERS MATTER

Leaders matter. We need good leadership, for our workplaces, our countries and our communities. Good leaders can make or break a workplace. Good leadership can steer a dental practice around and grow their team in a multitude of ways.

Did you know that a 2018 Gallup survey revealed that only 22% of teams believe their leaders have any clear direction for their company? That's not a lot of people feeling they have good leaders to learn from.

But it's not just staff that want leadership. People want to learn how to be leaders. In fact, 71% of millennials leave their job within two and three years if they feel their leadership skills aren't being maximised.

We not only need leaders, we need to learn how to become leaders. We need to nurture leadership in our youth and also consider that older team members still want to grow and explore leadership. As said by Johann Wolfgang von Goethe, "Treat people as if they were what they ought to be, and you help them become what they are capable of being."

11

WHY YOU MUST BE ONBOARD WITH THE HOLISTIC MOVEMENT IN THE DENTAL INDUSTRY

"Build a certain type of spirit, a certain type of mentality, that will reflect a certain type of character."
– Dr Kinnar Shah

DENTAL TRENDS

It is important to stay connected with emerging dental trends and the future of the dental industry, including the ageing population demographics, number of Dentists (and dental careers) and changing technology.

THE NEW WAY OF DOING BUSINESS IS HOLISTIC

I am not talking about ditching fluoride, going all natural and telling your clients to pull with coconut oil here. Traditional dentistry focuses on teeth, gums, jaws, the area of the head and neck affected by the mouth, and treatments that tend to be more reactive (fillings, crowns and so on). When I say holistic, I am talking about focusing on the entire person (the 'whole' body) to keep their overall health at its optimum level and include environmental (work, sleep, emotional) and nutritional elements that contribute to and support a patient's lifestyle.

It includes looking at the health of each patient's mouth to see whether it is disease-free; if decay or gum disease is present and affecting the vitality and structure of each tooth; whether anything is fractured or broken; the patient's oral hygiene habits; along with desired outcomes such as whitening, straightening, crowns, and so forth. It is expanding the longevity of the existing framework so that the patient can extend the lifespan of their existing teeth from 50 years to 80 years. This is so that when they are well into their elderly years, they can still enjoy their favourite steak. I have been to many nursing homes to service and deliver dentures, and it is sad that they cannot enjoy their meals.

It is beginning the journey of longevity with the younger

and emerging generations. It embraces educating those who are not looking after their teeth as much as they could be, so they can pivot their habits to achieve better mouth health and have a smile of confidence.

It is looking at the lifestyle of a patient and identifying any symptoms and warning signs for a range of diseases and conditions and advising preventative measures:

- Are they taking medications that reduce saliva flow?

- Do they work in a highly stressed environment? (They may have increased prevalence of sleep apnoea.)

- Do they grind not only at night, but clench/grind during the day sitting in front of a computer or sit hunched in front of the computer?

- Do they have poor oral hygiene? (This can contribute to diabetes, endocarditis, cardiovascular disease, osteoporosis, oral cancers, pregnancy and birth complications, pneumonia).

And through holistic dentistry you are creating a relationship for life through the wellbeing, care and nurturing of each individual patient.

MAKING THE SHIFT FROM HIGH VOLUME TO HOLISTIC

Looking to make the shift from high volume to holistic but want to know how to make it a smooth transition? As you will have read through the book, a holistic dental practice is preventative rather than reactive, which means you can say goodbye to:

- Patients who only see a Dentist when there is a problem.

- The appointment book frequently running late as treatments go over their allocated time slot.

- Patients who do not prioritise their dental health.

- Patients delaying treatment for financial reasons (willing to spend to fix a problem only).

- Patient anxiety, as patients get to know the team and trust the work being performed (allowing continuity of care).

Here is a list of what to consider for the shift to holistic dentistry:

Financial

- Assess where you are financially, your services and existing patient demographics.

- Decide on the income you would like the practice to generate.

- Identify revenue opportunities.

- Decide which services the practice offers going forward (including new services that are emerging trends).

- The efficiency of the dental chair.

- Treatment prices.

- Patient demographics moving forward.

Operational

- Assess the infrastructure required to deliver the new services (and costs, including equipment, time, labour, and training).

- Assess whether the practice needs to increase or reduce staff numbers due to a change in services, and/or operating days/times, and plan for future growth.

- Identify what the appointment book will look like moving forward and the processes needed to support the booking process.
- Create a strategy for rolling out the new plan.

Leadership

- Assess clinician production abilities and potential.
- Produce goals for the principal partner and clinicians.
- Understand the auxiliary team capabilities, potential and development.

Patient experience

- Listing the patient journey:
- Transitioning patients from the reactive dental to preventative.
- Identifying the New Patient journey.
- Build rapport.

- Deliver the treatment plan.

- Remain connected and build the relationship with the patient in between appointments.

Culture
- Audit the culture of the organisation and staff dynamics.

- Audit the codes of conduct, human resources policies in alignment with industry guidelines.

Technology
- Audit existing software and support capabilities to streamline processes, (reminders, SMS, email, and so on).

- Audit the practice website and update it in alignment with new operations.

- Training for new/updated processes.

Marketing
- Consider how you market your practice through website, SEO, social media.

The key to success is ensuring each staff member is aligned with the new direction of the practice. From experience, you can expect individuals who are not aligned at the onset of the change to take three years to integrate (if they do not leave). It can take three years to fully comprehend how the change can benefit their career as well as the practice. It may be that their personal values are out of alignment, that they are used to working the traditional way, they may be straight out of university and unable to grasp the concept, or they could be someone who understands the structure but does not know how to get there. This is where time is needed to train and mentor repeatedly.

Any time a new Dentist joins the practice, they spend a minimum of four weeks training, and they do not see any new patients until they understand the holistic model because that is where it starts, building rapport at a patient's first visit.

LET'S WORK TOGETHER

Are you looking to take your practice to the next level? Do you have staff who would benefit from coaching and mentoring? Or do you need assistance in the strategy and implementation of change? Do your processes and guidelines need updating? Does your auxiliary team need training? Have you been unable to change the culture successfully? Or do you need someone to find the right staff for you?

Connect with me to discuss how I can help you shift to holistic dentistry in an easy and stress-free way so that you too can grow and sustain a successful practice. I can also assist you with recruiting new staff.

Book a free 30 min call with Susie at
thedentalconcierge.com.au

ABOUT THE AUTHOR

Susie Raso is an NLP and dental practice performance coach, who practices NLP, timeline therapy, and hypnosis. She has over 25 years' experience working in the dental industry, helping dental practitioners live the dream of owning their own successful practices.

As a child, Susie loved going to the Dentist. The staff were always so lovely and made her feel at ease. From a young age, she knew she wanted to help others, and becoming a dental nurse was the perfect way to do just that.

Susie is self-motivated and loves getting results, whether she's helping a client through their anxiety or assisting a team member upskill and dare to be the best they can.

During her time in the dental industry, she noticed a huge unmet need among highly qualified Dentists, who tended to build their businesses around their own abilities to produce results. Inspired by the entrepreneurial practice owners she worked with, Susie recognised that most small business owners struggled to envision their businesses as separate from themselves. Combining her knowledge as a qualified trainer educator and NLP practitioner with her extensive dental experience and qualifications, she set out to help practice owners train, delegate, and build resilient teams so they could achieve the freedom they were looking for.

In her time getting to know and support practice owners throughout Australia, she has learned that while you and your practice are unique, for owners wanting to grow a practice, the challenges and frustrations aren't.

Outside of her professional life, Susie loves a good, challenging game of netball, lifting weights, travelling, reading, and spending quality time with her family.

thedentalconcierge.com.au

ACKNOWLEDGEMENTS

Thank you to my beautiful mother, Carmela. Without your love and support I would not be where I am today. I love how you always had the strength as a single mother to carry on with life and support my brother and me. You gave us great opportunities despite your own pain, always smiling and showing me how to carry on. You are the strongest and most courageous woman I know. When I am lost, you find me. When I am down, you bring me up. Everything I am today, the strong woman that I am, and the love I give to my son and family, reflects you.

Thank you to my partner Angelo for loving me and always supporting my view and life vision. I appreciate how you give me the freedom to be my own person and are super helpful when I am in need. You always listen, and your strength helps me to keep me going when I am hard on myself. Babes, I love you to the moon and back. You know how to make me laugh and remind me of my own words, "Everything will be okay." And most of all, thank you for reminding me to have fun (SuAnge).

Thank you to my dear friend Roberta for being a great mentor in my life for over 20 years. Your knowledge, strength and passion have helped me over the years. Your dental knowledge and skills refined me as an "A grade" Dental Assistant.

Thank you – my little baby boy, Elio; you have completed me. You bring so many exciting new things to us. I have thanked God and counted my blessings every day since I knew you were coming into this world. You are a beautiful, handsome and delightful surprise; I could not be more grateful. When you came into the world, everything in my life aligned, and you gave me direction and purpose. Even though you are so young right now, I would like to thank you for being inspiring and being the spark igniting the rest of my life. Ti Amo, Cookie!

Thank you to my mentors Greg and Michelle, for understanding me as a person and seeing my true potential. Thank you for allowing me the freedom I needed to grow and develop into a great leader. The business skills I have fostered from you are a true example of what it takes to have a High Performance Dental Team.

ENDNOTES

1. Bellet, C, De Neve, J & Ward G 2019, 'Does employee happiness have an impact on productivity?', *Saïd Business School WP*, vol 13, viewed 9 August 2022, http://dx.doi.org/10.2139/ssrn.3470734.

2. American Dental Association 2015, *2015 dentist well-being survey report*, report, viewed 9 August 2022, https://ebusiness.ada.org/assets/docs/32944.PDF.

3. Kay, EJ & Lowe, JC 2008, 'A survey of stress levels, self-perceived health and health-related behaviours of UK dental practitioners in 2005', *British Dental Journal*, vol 204, no 11, viewed 9 August 2022, https://doi.org/10.1038/sj.bdj.2008.490.

4. Gee, NR, Reed et al. 2019, 'Observing live fish improves perceptions of mood, relaxation and anxiety, but does not consistently alter heart rate or heart rate variability', *International Journal of Environmental Research and Public Health*, vol 16, no 17, viewed 9 August 2022, https://doi.org/10.3390/ijerph16173113.

5. Atlassian, *Company values*, web page, viewed 9 August 2022, https://www.atlassian.com/company/values.

6. NLP Academy, *What is NLP?*, web page, viewed 9 August 2022, https://www.nlpacademy.co.uk/what_is_nlp/.

www.ingramcontent.com/pod-product-compliance
Lightning Source LLC
Chambersburg PA
CBHW050359120526
44590CB00015B/1747